SECRETS OF THE ACHIEVER MIND

CREATE YOUR OWN SUCCESS

RAHUL THAKUR

Copyright © Rahul Thakur
All Rights Reserved.

This book has been published with all efforts taken to make the material error-free after the consent of the author. However, the author and the publisher do not assume and hereby disclaim any liability to any party for any loss, damage, or disruption caused by errors or omissions, whether such errors or omissions result from negligence, accident, or any other cause.

While every effort has been made to avoid any mistake or omission, this publication is being sold on the condition and understanding that neither the author nor the publishers or printers would be liable in any manner to any person by reason of any mistake or omission in this publication or for any action taken or omitted to be taken or advice rendered or accepted on the basis of this work. For any defect in printing or binding the publishers will be liable only to replace the defective copy by another copy of this work then available.

*This book is dedicated to those people who are
dedicated to achieving extraordinary success in life.*

Contents

PREFACE

Preface

In 2012, I was depressed, and it was difficult to find the reason. I was the only sad person among my friends. I just wanted to avoid being alone. Many times suicidal thoughts came into my mind. I usually went to parties. Many times I threw parties to avoid loneliness. The worst thing was, I didn't know the reason for my depression. It is really hard to find a solution when you don't know the problem, so how can you find the solution?

So I decided to find out the reason for depression and I started observing things. I remembered my school days and I asked myself why I was happy on those days. I have been remembering my school days daily and was thinking about the joy of that time. Furthermore, I was deeply analyzing the situation and used to think about every aspect of life which I had in my school days. Besides, I observed so deeply and after long observation, I found that in my school days I had a purpose for life. I wanted to become a successful entrepreneur. Moreover, I was working for that by completing my education and there was a hope that after school I will be an entrepreneur. But after school, I was not doing anything to achieve my goal. I was distracted from my goal, and I was fooling myself by doing parties.

I understood the reason for my depression, it was a purposeless life, a life without a goal, I deviated from my goal. As I realized it, I decided to work towards my goal. I stopped wasting my time at parties and other useless entertainment. Because I had realized that those are all temporary satisfactions, **only success gives real and long-lasting satisfaction in life**. I researched deeply about the secrets of success. I read thousands of books and researched a lot about successful people. Besides, I read many religious books to know the secret of success. Moreover, I read thousands of successful people's biographies, to know their secrets of success. Besides, I researched many successful people, talked to them, and asked about their secrets of life. I found many common learnings. One of the **most common things was, they all had a goal.** They all had a big goal in their lives, and they all knew some common ways to achieve that goal. So I implemented their teachings and ways in my life, and it drastically changed my life. I started working towards my goal. After 2 months I got out of a long depression. It worked like magic for me. **I found the secret of real happiness, it's the achievement of goals, success.** Yes, it is! People who always set goals in their lives and accomplish them, (or are in the process of accomplishing goals). They always stay happy. **Let's talk about the most peaceful and happiest people in the world. They are monks, why are they always happy and peaceful? Because they work to achieve their goals.**

So after knowing this secret, and working towards my goal I became a happy and enthusiastic person and I never look back. Now I live a happy life. I never worry. I have accomplished every goal of my life. Furthermore, I am working to achieve my future goals. **I got lucky to know the secrets of achieving goals.** I proudly say that I accomplish every goal in my life.

I helped many people by sharing techniques and ways of achieving their goals. I have benefited thousands of people with these secret teachings. Thousands of people achieved their goals in life by knowing these secrets. **I felt a need to share this knowledge with the world, I realized that everyone who wants to achieve big goals deserves this secret.** But due to limited availability, I can't teach everyone by myself. **There is a need to tell everyone who wants to achieve a goal, should have this precious knowledge. I felt that no one should suffer as I suffered to know these secrets.** So I compiled every secret in this book. **So you also can achieve great success in your life by reading and implementing the principles of this book.** You will accomplish your every goal as soon as you read and implement the learnings of this book. This book is for you to accomplish your goal. This book is a step-by-step process to achieve your goal and happiness. You can expect extraordinary growth in your life after implementing the secrets of this book.

Part One

FORGET OBSTACLES

I
Forget To Start

This lesson is about some common myths and beliefs that everyone should leave here before reading the second lesson. Before starting something good. First, you should throw out the garbage from your mind. An empty mind is a thousand times better than a mind with garbage. So first we are going to empty our minds to know great things, and we will throw away wrong beliefs and unnecessary things. So in this lesson, we will know how to get rid of the garbage that society gives us. We must clean up our minds and return them to their owners to grow in our life.

Give up

Let's start with the easiest thing in the world. The easiest thing in the world is becoming a loser because you have to do nothing to become a loser. Then why don't you become a loser of negativity? Don't dwell in negative thoughts, lose them immediately. Your mind can have many random thoughts daily and many of them could be negative thoughts, you do not have to let your mind focus on them, let them come and go out. Become A loser of bad habits by not repeating them, a loser of limited mindset, a loser of self-doubts (by giving up on them), a loser of poverty by becoming rich, Loser of procrastination. Nobody is born with this garbage. This is unwanted garbage imposed on your mind.

The mind is capable of generating new thoughts. To keep new thoughts, you need space to keep them, so first, clean your mind, throw out the garbage. It is important and the first step towards success. We should give up on useless thoughts because they do not belong to us. Humans take this from others' minds. **It is the same as collecting garbage from your neighbor's house and storing it in your house**. Negative people's minds are dustbins. They have stored garbage for years. They have a habit of passing this garbage to others' minds.

So in this lesson, we will discuss how to get rid of mental obstacles. It should be our first step to free our minds from unnecessary burdens. You have to leave all mentioned mental obstacles here and move further. I am going to clean your mind with facts and examples, so leave these mental obstacles here and move further in your life with the learnings. **To run fast, first, you need to throw out the extra weight of garbage.**

Wrong Conditioning with Wrong People

All humans experience some good and bad experiences. This is the process of human life. Bad experiences of failure may teach a lesson to a person if he learns from them and proves his learning by becoming successful. But a bad experience is completely worthless if a person doesn't learn from it and doesn't become successful. Despite this, some people pass their bad experiences to others to show mankind's limits(but always remember, a loser can show only a loser's limits). They discourage other people from their bad experiences. They try to negatively program other people's minds with their bad experiences. Furthermore, they say words like life is not easy, money doesn't grow on trees, or I failed, so you will also fail. These losers always underestimate other people, and they try to measure other people's abilities with their parameters. They have a Superiority complex(A superiority complex is a belief that your abilities or accomplishments are somehow dramatically better than other people's. People with a superiority complex may be condescending, smug, or mean to other people who don't agree with them). They try to program other people according to their limits. They try to make others feel bad. These are the frustrated people, they envy others' achievements.

You don't have to listen to their advice. Their bad experiences don't matter because there is zero learning in their bad experience. They are losers, and can only teach you to be a loser. They want others to join them to become losers.

Person A's bad experience is garbage for person B. **Why feel like a loser, without even becoming one?** You do not need the loser's experience. Do not let other people condition your mind negatively with their bad experiences. Losers are only case studies. To learn from their case studies, don't have to listen to their advice. You don't have to do what they did, you don't have to think like them. You don't have to be in their company. Furthermore, you do not have to let them influence you.

Nobody takes cancer from relatives and friends, then why take mental cancer of bad experience and advice from them. Their Advice is cancer. **It is the same as taking fitness advice from a 150 kg person. "Never take fitness advice from a 150 kg person and never take advice for life from a loser".** Take advice only from achievers who have accomplished great success. Take advice from the winner because they know how to win. If you don't know any winners, then listen to winners on News channels and Social Media. The advice of legends like Bill Gates and Warren Buffett.

Bad Luck or Destiny

You may have heard people saying, 'it is bad luck, 'it is Monday, it will be a bad day, 'oh no! Black cat now it can ruin my day; 'It is Friday the thirteenth, it will be the worst day of the year'. Don't you think that these kinds of people are just looking for a reason to ruin the day?

Egoistic people are less likely to accept their errors, that's why they always blame others or situations for their failure. If their ego does not let them find the reason for their failure, then they start blaming luck and other factors.

Bad luck doesn't exist, Nobody can define it exactly because it doesn't exist. These concepts are used by losers to hide their errors. Achievers always accept their errors and learn from them. Achievers never blame others for their errors. Achievers don't hide behind the board of bad luck.

Who introduced these dogmas?

These dogmas were introduced by superstitious people. People who believe that dark magic is behind every bad thing happening. Every wise man knows that there is no existence of black magic. We know that these things were introduced by superstitious people to hide their errors.

To become an achiever, it is necessary to understand that there is no bad luck. Nothing can stop you from accomplishing your goal. It's not about good luck or bad luck, so forget about the luck and work to achieve your goal. You can create your luck by working. Never let this garbage occupy your brain. **"You have only good luck and you are the luckiest person on this planet"**. Believe it because it is true.

Destiny

Infinite Possibilities

You may have heard about Nostradamus' predictions. Many people believe in his predictions. Many people believe that his predictions are 100% true. Some fake people use his predictions to run their propaganda. Whenever they want to show superiority of their fake guru or their prediction, they use Nostradamus' predictions for reference. But if you deeply analyze Nostradamus' predictions, You'll find that these are only fantasies because Nostradamus had not defined time and date in his predictions. He hadn't specified that this prediction is for which particular date and year. You'll see that people link his predictions with every event which they want to show as pre-defined, or where they want to link one situation with another to show their credibility. They find every event in Nostradamus' prediction to favor them. News channels show those predictions to increase their TRP.

Have you ever read Nostradamus predictions? Nostradamus' predictions are like "one man will lead the world, he will be born in a region where 4 rivers merge and form a larger river". Does it make any sense to a wise man? Are those predictions useful in any manner?

This world has infinite possibilities. Everything that one can imagine is possible to be true in this world. For example: If someone predicts that I am going to die tomorrow in a road accident. And the next day I decided to stay home to save my life. So I will not die in a road accident and prediction will fail. It means I have changed my destiny, which means I am the creator of my destiny. So what is the relevance of prediction when we are the creator of your life? I proved predictions wrong by staying at home. That is why predictors never specify days and times, they are wise enough which is why they never mention the date and time of their predictions.

They predict obvious things like Rahul you're going to die one day, obviously man! It is a fact, and it doesn't need prediction. Similarly, they predict tsunamis and other natural disasters, but they never mention dates because they know the fact that one day, obviously there will be a tsunami in the ocean region. Everyone knows the fact that in the ocean region, tsunamis are natural and spontaneous. Predictors are making people fool.

If someone predicts future events and does not mention the dates, then it is only a fantasy. Predictor well knows the fact that this universe has infinite possibilities and one day his words definitely will become true. For example: If I predict that one day every human will fly, we will fly individually. At that time we humans will not need any car or bike to travel, everyone will fly. So here if I don't mention dates, because I know that one day it is going to be a fact. Humans will invent a technology where we humans will fly. That technology will use solar energy or any natural energy and will be auto chargeable. It will take energy from the environment without any inconvenience to the user. This technology will not need any power station to charge. This technology will be superfast and time-saving.

So it was my prediction and I believe it to be 100 percent true one day. Because I know this universe has infinite possibilities and one day we will have technology where it will be so eco-friendly and not even use electricity to fly. (Electricity is one type of energy. Universe has many forms of energy, we can discover more forms of energy, and we can use them too without converting that energy into the form of heat and electricity. We are just lacking the technology of the use of energy in its pure form. But one day we humans will learn to use energy in its pure form).

So based on the infinite possibilities, I believe that my prediction will be true one day. But it doesn't mean that I have supernatural powers. No, not at all, I predicted it because I know this universe has infinite possibilities and science is growing rapidly.

Astrologers predict the future by date of birth by looking at the directions of stars. They do not have an answer to a single question: about 1605 babies are born every day. Let's take the example of billionaire Mark Zuckerberg. His date of birth is May-14-1984, he is a Billionaire and many people were born on the same day, same location, and in the same city. Now, according to astrology logic, they all should have the same luck because stars do not change their direction much within a day. By this logic, they all should be billionaires. But I don't know another single billionaire, who was born on that day. Rather some of them would be beggars and obviously, the maximum of them would be middle class.

So it is clear that our actions create our destiny. We are the creator of our destiny. **"Lord Krishna Says One's Karma creates one's destiny"**. We can enjoy the results of our actions, We are the creators of our destiny. Furthermore, we can have a lot, we can create our fortune. The universe has plenty to give everyone. Throw out garbage from your mind and clear your mind. **"Always remember your only destiny is success"**

Limits

Society always told me "Spread as many sheets as you can". You may have heard these kinds of lines. But believe me, these lines are created by losers because they want you to stay with them. This is a trap, don't fall in this trap, They can only tell you their limits, not yours. You may have noticed that people are always eager to tell you about themselves. People rarely listen to others because they are ignorant. Do they do the same when they talk about limits? People measure you by their parameters (Their limited thinking) but their tools only show their limits. You don't need to fit yourself in their parameters.

Jim Hines

It was said that it is impossible to sprint 100 meters in less than 10 seconds. People used to say that it is beyond human limits. But American Jim Hines became the first man to run the100 meters in less than 10 seconds in1968. After this record by Jim, many sprint runners broke this record because they raised their parameters. They have seen a limitless person, and they also wanted to become one. They understood it is possible to run 100 meters within 10 seconds.

Bumblebee

The bumblebee has smaller wings in her body ratio and according to laws of physics, it is impossible to fly for bumblebees. But the funniest thing about bumblebees is they don't read physics. But they enjoy flying beyond the physics laws. What if they had read physics, maybe they could never fly. We, humans, limit everything because we are programmed in such a way by our society.

Limits only exist in the human mind, throw them out from your mind and become limitless. You are born limitless, so stay limitless. Only losers have limits. A loser's limit is an outcome; they can't go beyond that.

Hard Work And Success

In our modern society, a child has always been taught that he has to work hard to be successful, but if you think it to be true then you'll have to work till you die. If it were true, then a donkey would be the wealthiest being in this world, no one works harder than a donkey. A donkey works for his entire life, but nobody pays a donkey for his work. His owner only feeds him to make him able to do work. The owner keeps his earnings. We all do the same, we all work hard to achieve success, without understanding that success doesn't come with only hard work. **Success comes with smart work, work done in the right direction at the right time with your 100% effort.**

Start the journey, you'll be an expert in the journey

This is the biggest lie that has ever been told to us, "start without preparation". This statement destroys you in real-life. This statement doesn't have any relation with real-life's successful people.

You should prepare before you start anything. Riding a bike without knowledge can cost you your life (or at least a leg), but taking life-changing actions without knowledge and preparation can destroy you and your family's lives. You should start by learning. If you learn and do proper research before starting, then the chances of failure are less. **"Nobody goes to the examination hall with that attitude. "Sit in the examination hall, and you will learn during the exam".**

Sir Isaac Newton

Newton was one of the early investors in the South Sea Company, which was founded in 1711 to trade with Spanish America. In 1720, the company bagged a deal to manage British government debt. As soon as the news spread, the price of the South Sea stock started soaring.

Newton, who was then the warden of the Royal Mint in London, wisely chose to book profits in April and pocketed a handsome gain of about £20,000, a princely sum in those years.

As the euphoria around the stock kept on inching higher with every passing day, Newton could not resist the temptation of buying the hottest stock in town once again. According to the research paper, he invested nearly all his money into the venture in June that year.

The man, who developed the calculus and formulated the laws of motion, ended up buying the stock almost at the peak of the bubble. The stock underwent a precipitous collapse in September, most likely because investors began to realize their profit expectations were unrealistic. By October, the stock was worth less than a quarter of its peak price. "By mid-1721, Newton's net worth was down to about £20,000; he had lost all his early profits and a good bit more besides.

"Even Newton failed without preparation" is the importance of preparation".

Keynotes

- Bad luck doesn't exist, only infinite possibilities exist.
- Limits only exist in people's minds, they tell you their limits.
- You can extend your sheets as much as you want.
- Smart work makes you successful.

- The best way to start is by learning.

II

Choose Carefully

Every human has the power to choose. Choices make a difference in life. The right choice at the right time can make you extremely successful. A wrong choice can destroy you. Choosing good habits can make you a hero, and choosing bad habits can make you zero. "A human is the product of his habits, and his life is the outcome of his choices". As we are the wisest being on earth, we have a lot of great options to choose from with our wisdom. There we have options to select good habits and bad habits. You can choose to drink alcohol and at the same time, can choose to read books. Both of these choices are going to become habits, and these habits are going to make a huge difference in your life.

You can choose between meditation, yoga, or playing violent games. You can add value to your life, or you can choose to play online games in the morning to ruin your entire day and waste time. This shows results in the compound. On one side, playing online games is not going to add any value in life, and on the other side, meditation will make a person wiser and calm.

So here we will discuss some bad choices that achievers avoid.

Environment

You may think that choices are natural and part of my personality, I can't change my personality so easily. So foremost, you need a cohering personality to achieve a goal. Creating or changing a personality is not a difficult thing; you just have to create an environment that forces you to create your desired personality. The human mind creates a personality according to the environment, the human brain is adaptable.

Lesbians' Jail

There is a famous female jail and the culture of jail is very different. In that jail, women try to attract each other by singing and dancing. An environment is created there. Being a lesbian is normal at that place. The awkward thing about that jail is that all the prisoners were straight before going to prison. They had families and husbands. But they became lesbians after spending some time in that jail. After releasing from jail, maximum of them, divorce their existing partner and live with their new lesbian partners.

Whenever a straight female goes into jail, the females of that jail try to impress her. She feels awkward for some days, but after some days she feels that it is normal because she sees it daily and everyone is doing it there. Her mind tries to adjust her according to the environment. After some days, her mind adjusts her personality to fit in that environment. She becomes lesbian too. Every prisoner becomes lesbian after spending some days in that jail.

Now it is important to understand that there are many female jails in the world but only that jail has these kinds of activities. Why so? Because only that jail has the environment where females feel natural for being a lesbian. That environment where every straight woman becomes a lesbian also forces a straight woman's mind to become lesbian. Her mind tries to create a common floor and tries to adjust her personality according to the environment. It is because of the environment of that jail. (For reference, you can watch the National Geographic's Taboo, they have also made a documentary on this topic)

We all know that gender matters a lot for an individual. A person's self-image starts with his gender. It is enough to understand the power of the environment, the environment can force a person to change his self-image. It can force them to change their identity. This is the power of the environment, and this is how the environment affects a person's life. A loser environment can make a person a loser, and a winner's environment can make a person a winner.

Create Progressive Environment

You have to create a progressive environment so that your mind can work to adjust your personality accordingly. ("Even an atheist person feels religious when he goes into the temple, church, mosque, etc. because there is an environment of religious divine") It is necessary to create a positive environment around us and avoid negative people. Remove losers from your life. Remove those people who try to demean you every time. Change your environment to develop an achiever's personality because having an achiever's personality is as important as having a goal to achieve.

Friend Circle

Friends play an indispensable role in a person's environment. You should choose friends carefully because friends also create a huge impact on you. Your environment is mostly influenced by your friend circle. So you must create a friend circle where all of your friends are focused on their goals and want to achieve big goals in life. (The secret of the millionaire mind book has addressed this topic in detail. The author says that tell him your four friends, and he can tell you your future). You should avoid the company of those friends who always make you feel like a loser. Because those friends will never let you grow, they ruin your environment.

Lord Krishna says in Geeta "bad company is an ignorance and a wise man always avoids it to grow"

Choose Carefully

We should make choices carefully. Because every time we choose, we may choose to be pessimistic or optimistic. We choose everywhere. The right choice is very important. Right choices lead to more right choices, and wrong choices lead to more wrong choices.

When a person starts smoking, he tends to be more likely to drink alcohol. A smoker is more likely to take drugs as compared to a non-smoker. A thief is more likely to become a killer because he has already stepped-in in crimes. When a person smokes for the first time, he feels so bad for it, he believes it to be wrong, but after some time his mind normalizes it, he feels that nothing is wrong with this. His mind has convinced him. Now, his mind is less likely to oppose him from drinking liquor, because he has already normalized his addictions. It is a Kaizen step towards bad habits.

A bad choice leads to more bad choices. Humans feel instant pleasure by smoking and drinking, humans feel rewarded by smoking and drinking. And he does that more for more rewards. The human brain releases dopamine after smoking and drinking, this dopamine makes him feel pleasure. That is why he wants to repeat it again and again. Similarly, a thief's brain releases dopamine when he steals money, he recognizes it as an achievement, and he wants to achieve more. A person should never choose the wrong option because it will lead him to choose more bad things, and this is how a person chooses every wrong thing in his life.

So whenever you are about to choose something wrong, stop it before taking action, don't let it go ahead, and lead your other choices. Always choose good things and good options, so they will lead you to more good choices and decisions.

Games

Violence games: These days, these games are getting popular. The main idea behind these games is violence, looting, stealing, killing people, and battle. These games are programming the player's mind, to create his violent personality. These games send a message to the player's mind that looting and stealing are normal and cool. They start to believe that looting is normal. These games subconsciously program a person's mind with violence.

These kinds of games fill a lot of garbage in the human mind. It makes humans feel that loot and violence are cool. It kills a person's productivity. These games are responsible for the increased rate of crimes and suicidal cases. People play these games for pleasure and slowly, without realizing it, these games fill their minds with hate violence and crime. An average teen spends 7 hours and 22 minutes a day on a mobile phone. These 7 hours and 22 minutes are more than enough to condition his mind.

We as a responsible society must take strict actions against these games. These games are normalizing violence in our minds. We all know that there are many illegal sex games available on illegal websites, but they are illegal at least. Their selling is banned in the public domain. Because those games promote rapes. They can cause rapes. But why don't we think in the same way for games where violence is cool, where stealing, killing, and looting are part of winning the game? When our society believes that sex games can promote rape. Then how can we think that games with the concept of violence will not promote violence, looting, and murders? Is murder not a crime? Why don't we demand and protest to ban these games? If we will let normalize these games then definitely after some time sex and rape games will be the part of our mobile phones, where people will be rewarded for doing rape and kidnapping in the game.

These games grab the full attention and emotions of the player. The player can talk to his friends, and they plan to kill the opponent team, they plan for looting. They are not just playing a game, but they are involved in the game. They are 100% focused on the game. Furthermore, they are feeling every move while playing. These games are more dangerous than sex games because they fully include a person.

If we do nothing to stop this kind of crap, then after 10-15 years when these teens will be young. At that time, consequences will be more visible. We will have useless adults whose minds will be conditioned to only play those games, and their qualities will be more and more killings and looting in the games. Those people's minds will be conditioned as looting and killing normal. These games have side effects that can lead a nation towards downfall. These kinds of games will only give losers to the world, this kind of environment can never give achievers to the world.

These games have many disadvantages, but I am mentioning some individual side effects that every player has to face.

These games waste time.

These games are also bad for the eyes and health.

Children are not playing outdoor games because of these games. Children are not studying.

Subconsciously, it can drag a person into depression. In the beginning,

The player thinks that these games are helping him to be relaxed. But this is a slow poison and slowly the player starts to feel depressed because these games play with human psychology. Many of them commit suicide because of continuously losing the battle in games. Some children first steal money from their parents to buy weapons in the game, and then they commit suicide out of fear of face-off with their parents. These are the teachings that the game is teaching them. We can see the impact of these games, first players steal money to play the game because they are programmed by the game for stealing money, and then they commit suicide. Games are programming them that killing and dying are very normal. These games are spoiling our society. These types of games must be banned because it is creating a useless generation. It will create a worse future for mankind. Our future generation will not be intelligent and physically fit if this trend continues. This generation of children are facing serious issues like disc problems in their early

20s, what can we expect from them in the future. We will only have losers in the future if we don't stop these games right now.

We all know the mental effects of gaming, to recall it, you may read the consequences of the BLUE WHALE game, that game mentally pressurized many people to commit suicide. At that time we used to daily read the news many teenagers commit suicide because of the games.

I assume that a person earns money by playing games. But what value that game is going to add to his life. If the game got banned, then he won't have any skill of earning money. He will have an unfit body too. So it is neither a stable source of earning.

Achievers never waste their time playing these kinds of games. An achiever should always avoid these games to be productive. If an achiever has to spend time on mobile, he spends it by doing something productive and learning.

Music

Sad songs can make you a pessimistic person. Achievers never listen to sad songs and those ugly trances. Sad songs fill a person's mind with sorrows, sorrows are a toxic emotion. As you know, our environment creates a huge impact on our personality and our personality leads us to accomplish our goal, so by listening to sad songs a person only ruins his environment and mood. Sad songs have only negative words, and those words become affirmations in your mind. It leads to a pessimistic personality, and pessimistic people do not achieve much in their life. Avoid "broken heart" songs, avoid crying songs, they are nothing, just ugly creations. An Achiever starts his day with some good music, some religious music, meditation music. In the morning, you should listen to soft music. It boosts productivity. Don't listen to meaningless music because it fills garbage in the mind, meaningless music conditions the mind meaninglessly. Positive music can boost your day and at the same time, a sad song can ruin your whole day.

I have a great example of music's impact on the human mind. There is a famous suicide song named **'Gloomy Sunday'**. In Vienna, a teenage girl drowned herself while clutching a piece of sheet music. In Budapest, a shopkeeper killed himself and left a note that quoted from the lyrics of the same song. In London, a woman overdosed while listening to a record of the song over and over. The piece of music that connects all these deaths is the notorious **'GLOOMY SUNDAY'** Nicknamed the "Hungarian suicide song," it has been linked to over one hundred suicides, including one of the men who composed it. Many TV channels and governments banned this song because of the suicides.

Sad songs send msg to the subconscious mind that this world is unfair. Nothing good happens with good people and many of these kinds of useless messages. As a result, a person always sees this world as an unfair place. **These people believe that life is a war, and I believe that they will be martyred in this war.**

Why do we listen to music? The answer is for mental peace, to be relaxed and calm but sad songs can never fulfill these purposes. Sad songs do the opposite; these songs steal mental peace and push you into depression.

A person who wants to be successful in life should avoid sad music. It's toxic and causes negativity in life. The choice is yours if you want to achieve your goal rapidly then you need to be a positive person. Positivity gives you the energy to do new stuff and do more than the capacity.

Movies

Movies also, play a critical role in creating a good environment. Movies leave a huge impact on a person's personality. Movies are time-wasters, and most of the ultra-successful people don't like to watch movies. However, if you have a habit of watching movies, then you can use it to create an awesome environment. Watch movies that encourage you to achieve goals, that motivates you, or where you can learn some good stuff.

We can see the impact of movies on children, who dwell in the role of the hero of the movie after watching a movie. They try to act like movie heroes. They observe things as movie heroes observe. Furthermore, they start acting like the main character of the movie. Their decisions and reactions depend on the character of that movie. They keep doing it until they watch a new movie.

I wanted to become a pilot in my childhood when I watched the' 'Pilot" movie. Then after some days, I watched the movie "Border". Then I decided to become a soldier. I have been acting like a soldier. I used to talk to my mother like "Mom". Furthermore, I have to serve my nation first. If I martyr in war, you will be a proud mother of a martyred son. My mother laughed at my dialogues. After some days I watched the Diljale movie, and then I wanted to become "Shaka". But I didn't have Sonali Bendre.

Why did I do so? Because children show their emotions shamelessly. I was doing the same, I was showing the impact of the movies on me. If psychologists had measured the effect of movies on my mind, they would get the most accurate results. Children don't have a strict Identity, they follow the flow. But as we grow up, we build our strict identities.

Movies and TV shows play an important role in our mind's conditioning. Movies deeply affect a person's mind and thoughts. A normal person who isn't afraid of ghosts starts to be afraid of ghosts if he sees a horror movie. This is the impact of movies.

Devdas Syndrome

Here I have an awesome example of the movie Devdas released on the date of 1st January 1955. Devdas loved his childhood friend Paro, but couldn't marry her because she was poor and of a lower caste. The introverted, silent man did not know how to confront his family nor fight social prejudice and instead turned to drink, ultimately destroying himself.

This short story challenged the Indian government. Because Indian youth as big fans started drinking a lot of liquor. It was not a small issue, even the newspapers covered it. The Government of India was worried about this concern. It was spreading like an epidemic in India, It was called Devdas Syndrome (For reference search **Devdas syndrome** on Google).

Sharabi

The same happened when the Sharabi movie was released on 18 May 1984, people started following the lead actor's movie character in their real life and started drinking a lot without thinking for a second that it is just a movie. It also became a huge issue. Indian youth became a challenge. Because of these kinds of incidents, the government-mandated anti-alcohol and anti-smoking warnings below the smoking and drinking scenes.

If one watches movies where the end is bad, where the end shows poverty as a destination or the story of the movie shows that this world is so unfair, then his subconscious mind also starts to see the world as an unfair place.

Horror Movies' Impact

In 2016 the Blue Whale game got attention. This game caused thousands of suicides. That game had many challenges. Their last challenge was suicide. Do you know how they were convincing people to commit suicide? This all happened because they convinced people by creating an environment. **The fact about this game is that they also had a level where they challenged the player to watch horror movies and videos in isolation to drag the player into depression. Here you can understand the impact of watching the wrong movies and playing the wrong games.**

So watch only inspiring movies, biopics, and movies of billionaires' success stories like; "The Founder".These kinds of movies inspire a person to set a big goal and accomplish that. These movies give knowledge and motivation. These kinds of movies have a message about the importance of success. These movies help people to define their life goals and understand their life goals clearly.

Create a growing environment only for 45 days, and I challenge you, that your life and your thinking will change drastically. You will see the world differently. You will be more energetic, more goal-oriented, and more clear about your vision. It will also help a depressed person to come out of depression.

Keynotes

- Always choose well for yourself because you can.
- Create a good environment to grow in your life, your environment matters a lot.
- Always make good decisions, and choose well because good attracts more good.
- Don't play violent games, where killing and looting are cool.
- Never listen to sad and pessimistic music; it drains your positivity and energy.
- Never watch horror movies and movies with bad endings. It creates a negative impact on the mind.

III
MINDSET

Now we are moving towards developing an achievers mindset and here we will challenge the wrong thought process and wrong mindset

Self Doubt And Overthinking

Self Doubt

The subconscious mind has the power of multiplying things. If self-doubt will be sowed in the subconscious mind, then it will be multiplied. If self-confidence will be sowed in the subconscious mind, then it will be multiplied. The rule is simple: as soil grows what you sow in it, the mind also grows in multiple what you sow in it. The subconscious mind is the same as soil. It doesn't know whether you sowed flowers or bushes, it just multiplies and grows whatever is given to it. If self-doubt is sowed in the subconscious mind, it will be multiplied. So be careful while sowing anything in the subconscious mind. Humans are great without self-doubt. Self-doubt stops a person from taking action. It is impossible to achieve goals without taking action. Self-doubt leads to failure. Many people never try to take action to accomplish their goals because of self-doubt.

Overthinking

Overthinking is the reason for procrastination. Overthinking people can take several days to make a decision. After that, he regrets his decisions because he again overthinks about decisions. Overthinking can kill every awesome plan because overthinkers overanalyze, and they find problems with every solution. They look out for negative points first, and then they decide to not take any action on their plans. So a wise man always avoids overthinking and self-doubt to be successful.

You Are Perfect

You are part of the universal consciousness. **God has created you, and he has created everything perfect.** You are perfect! Yes, you are. You are the child of almighty god. Then why do self-doubt? Self-doubt is equal to doubting God's creation. **God has created everything perfect, we are no one to call ourselves imperfect.** We should not doubt God's plans. He always has better plans for every child.

Don't Work To Be Retired

Do you know what a loser wants in his life? Answer: is 'Retirement', a loser, works just to eat and feed his family. He is always ready to retire. The loser mindset always wants to work hard till the graduation of their children. They eagerly wait to make their child responsible. They just want to free themselves from their responsibilities. They want to see their children's marriage as soon as possible to be free from their responsibilities. Most of them quit their job as their children start earning. Their favorite line is: I earned for my entire life for my family now I will eat, and children will earn. That is why they always stay mediocre and losers in their life. That is why they don't achieve much in their lives.

Even they don't have enough to retire. They retire without achieving any goal in their life. They do not have a specific goal to achieve. They retire because they were always eager to do so. We need to understand the concept of retirement. A person should retire as soon as possible **"if he has earned enough to live a luxurious life for the rest of his life"**. There shouldn't be another reason for retirement.

What is the difference between humans and animals? Without having a vision for life, without setting and accomplishing goals in life. There is no difference between humans and animals. Animals also do sex, animals also have children, animals also take risks to eat good grass, animals (like the donkey, dog, buffalo) also work for others to feed themselves. All activities are similar. Then why do we call ourselves the wisest beings on the earth? This is the insult of our creator.

To be an achiever this mindset should be changed. Achievers never work to be retired. Achievers never run from their responsibilities. An achiever never stops until he accomplishes his goal. After accomplishing a goal, he sets another goal to grow in his life. Achievers have missions in their lives.

Poor Mindset

A poor mindset person thinks that expecting more and setting large goals are ridiculous and one should be satisfied with less. They are afraid of setting big goals for life because of fear of failure. Poor mindset people also demotivate other people, they seek out problems with every solution. If a person says something great in front of them, they seek out loopholes. Poor mindset people are poor in every aspect of life. They have a poor mindset about sports, money, singing, business, and everywhere. If someone is good at playing, these people advise them to earn some money instead of choosing a career in sports, they say that your limit is playing for the state level, don't think big. If someone is good at making money, then these people tell them that he is a loser because he is not good at sports. This is not because they are envied. These people never try anything to change their lives.

Nothing exists like satisfying in less because satisfaction comes after having more than enough. If someone has not achieved his goal and has not even tasted success, how can he say he is satisfied? How can satisfaction come in his life without abundance?

Only two things exist satisfaction and sacrifice. Losers replace sacrifice with satisfaction. Sacrifice means staying away from what you want.

So a person who wants to accomplish his goals in life should always set big goals in life, and he should always strive to accomplish them.

Achievers' mindset

Winners have a clear mindset, they have clear goals, and they work to achieve them. After achieving a goal, they always go for another goal. They have visions in their life. They have missions in their life, they live for a purpose. Bill Gates has achieved all his financial goals and now his mission is to add value to people's lives, and he is doing his best for it. He wants to make the earth a better place to live. He wants to cure millions of people in underdeveloped nations. He helps millions of people by doing charity. Achievers never quit on the name of their age. Age doesn't matter for achievers. Achievers never wait for anyone to take their responsibilities. They decide their responsibilities and complete that. Achiever is a mindset that everyone should have. There is no secret left, of becoming an achiever. I have already mentioned all of them in this book.

Achiever Ray Kroc

Ray Kroc spent most of the first decades of his professional career selling paper cups and milkshake machines. After discovering a popular California hamburger restaurant owned by Dick and Mac

McDonald, he went into business with the brothers and launched the McDonald's franchise in 1955. He was 52 when he started. He didn't retire until he got success in his life. He has a clear mindset of success. He has a clear goal of becoming an ultra-rich businessman. He worked for that until he got success. This is the way an achiever thinks.

You have to develop an achiever's mindset to be successful in your life. You can never be successful in life with self-doubt, poor mindset, and loser thinking, so to grow in life you need to remove these things from your life.

Keynotes

- Stop the habit of overthinking, it only offers bad things to you.
- Understand the difference between deep thinking and overthinking.
- Overthinking creates self-doubt and self-doubt is the biggest enemy of success.
- Never work for retirement, never try to be retired.
- Always set next-level goals for your life, retirement means purposeless life, so always set goals for the next level.
- Achievers never retire; they always work for a vision and mission.

IV
Rigidity

I was influenced by legendary investor Warren Buffett. I read all his favorite books, watched his biography, those good things, and researched everything about him. I watched all of his interviews. I started to create an environment where all the sources were teaching me about value investing. Main points I learned about value investing, investing for the long term, and not speculating in the market. That philosophy is right, but I took that wrong. In the beginning, I had only $1000 to invest. I doubled it within 6 months. I started to become comfortable with my situation. I was reading a lot of books, I was learning so many things about business. Inside me, I was thinking that I should not waste my time and efforts to do other things, I should only focus on the stock market. There is no other easy way to make money. This is the perfect thing that I am doing in my life. I have to do it for a lifetime. This is the best way and I don't need to hustle anywhere else, I should focus on only this source of income. I didn't realize that I had become a rigid person.

Cryptocurrency

In 2016 a new cryptocurrency Ethereum was gaining popularity. I was reading about cryptocurrencies. I was considering buying Ethereum because it was much cheaper than bitcoin. But before investing in cryptocurrency, I thought, I should listen to ace investors who have made their fortune by investing and trading. So I searched on the internet, the opinions of those people, they all were criticizing cryptocurrencies; some were saying what is the base behind the cryptocurrency? Many so-called value investing gurus on social platforms were saying that cryptocurrency has zero value, and it will collapse soon. Some were busy comparing cryptocurrencies with Tulip Mania (Thanks to SEBI now they have banned investment advisors' recommendations on unregulated instruments). So I assumed that it would be a waste of money to invest in cryptocurrency. Because everyone around me and people whom I believe were criticizing cryptocurrency. I became the biggest critic of cryptocurrency. I assumed that these types of assets are not safe, and they can become zero at any time. I had many points to criticize cryptocurrencies. I started criticizing cryptocurrency.

After some years, the Ethereum price hiked 1000 times, I realized that cryptocurrencies have given awesome returns to their investors. It has given multifold returns to investors. Ethereum never looked back, I realized my mistake. I had become a rigid person who did not want to adapt to change.

I had become a rigid person who did not want to adapt to the changes. My rigidity cost me a 500k USD opportunity loss. I missed the opportunity because I was rigid.

The lesson I learned from this incident

I realized that I was only trying to make other people responsible for my mistake. I had made a list of investors who were criticizing bitcoin. To convince me and blame others, I blamed the people who recommended not to invest in cryptocurrencies.

It was my mistake that I didn't invest in cryptocurrencies. Because of my rigid nature. (I am not here to promote bitcoin nor to criticize bitcoin. I am here just to tell you the side effects of rigidity). The rigidity can cause huge losses. A rigid person can never grow in his life. Rigidity never lets a person achieve his goals. Rigidity is the biggest obstacle between you and your goal. We are humans and our life and world are constantly changing. Success parameters have been changed. Ways to achieve goals have been changed. Even if the earth changes its position constantly, then why do humans stay rigid? Grow up and learn new skills, try every way to get success in life. Do everything that can get you near to your goal. Be a progressive man.

Achievers always stay ready to try new things. You should take a chance, at least take a risk on your 10 to 15 percent capital for faster return assets like bitcoin. If legends are right and these cryptocurrencies become zero, then you won't lose much. And if legends are wrong then it can make you a millionaire.

A rigid person feels offended with every new Idea. He may read books and listen to new ideas from others, but he never implements them because of rigidity. Rigidity doesn't let a person learn anything new in life. A rigid person can never believe in good things, he can not believe that good thing can happen so easily.

We, humans, are rigid by nature, rare humans are flexible. The best example is right-wing and left-wing, both have different ideologies and both do not agree with each other. Left-wingers never appreciate right-wingers' good decisions, and similarly, right-wingers never support left-wingers' good decisions. Right-wingers blame left-wingers for every problem, and left-wingers blame right-wingers for every problem. These two ideologies are the best examples of human's rigid nature.

Every time a rigid person sees something new, they say it will not last long, they may say old is gold, that's why I am Old and classy. But things don't work in this way. Goals don't give a damn about being royal and classy. Goals need appropriate actions for accomplishment. A goal doesn't care about the excuses. Only achievements matter.

A flexible approach is the best approach to accomplish goals. One should be flexible to accomplish his goals in life. Flexible people try new ways of success. Flexible people try every technique that can work for them. Flexible people don't have the attitude that I belong to this type of group. They support every right thing. If you want to earn money, then you should try every smart legal method to earn money. If someone says Nah! I don't like affiliate marketing, or I don't want to earn money from making videos on YouTube then he is making the biggest mistake. An achiever tries every way to achieve his goal. He never gives excuses that I don't know this, or I can't learn it. He learns everything, and he does not rely on other people's philosophies. He created his philosophy of success.

Success happens when you make the right decision at the right time. Success doesn't touch that person who neglects the opportunities because of his rigid nature. Opportunities don't come in an ignorant person's life because he is not able to see opportunities due to his negative thoughts about the new opportunities. **"Rigidity will not help you to reach your goal, but flexibility will"**

Achievers Adapt to Changes Easily

A person who does not adapt to changes, cannot be successful. This universe is changing continuously, Time, technology, and people are changing continuously then how can a person win a battle without changing his war techniques. A person who does not change, this world leaves him behind. **"This world is the fastest rocket, one can not chase it by running, so it's better to ride on it"**

A white bear cannot survive in the desert, and a camel cannot survive on the Everest mountains. But a human can survive in every climate, in every situation, even after some years we will set life on Mars.

"Strategies also have an expiry date if you don't upgrade them. Use of expired strategies are more harmful than expired medicines". Some people believe that they have the best strategies. They never try to upgrade their strategies.

Nokia

Nokia is the best example. They were market leaders after they launched the Nokia 1100 mobile, but they were kicked out of the market when they launched Android and Windows phones. This is because they didn't upgrade technology at the right time. They were expecting that customers would buy their phones because of their so-called brand value, but they didn't realize that their brand value is a fantasy. Nokia's strategy of ruling through brand value was outdated and consumers were updated. Value buyer segment Customers wanted more features and quality at a lower price, and the luxury customers shifted to the luxury brand Apple. Nokia was trying to compete based on their brand, but they forgot that they were outdated and were no more a reputed brand after the revolution of Android. They did not fit in any demand segment, they failed to target the middle class because the middle class was already getting more valuable phones at less prices. On the other hand, Nokia had no match with Apple. Nokia failed because they tried to rule the world with their old 20-year-old strategies, they never tried to understand the needs of the changing market. They didn't adapt to the change. They didn't understand the gap in the market. They were not offering anything better than other mobile companies, and their price was 1.5 times more than other mobile companies. This became the main reason for their failure. So here you can see that Nokia also had an old proven strategy, but they failed because they didn't adapt to the change, they didn't update their strategies. They didn't accept that the new world wanted value buying rather than old brand names.

This era does not care about what brand is old or new. It only cares about the quality and price of the product. A new world has left behind the old parameters of buying a product, where customers used to buy things from the house of an old brand. This era's customers need quality plus value for money. This is a huge change in customers' behavior. Only those companies survived who adapted themselves according to this change.

Old Friend

My old friend, as his introduction, also has an old programmed mind that he never wants to change. He refused to take advantage of online payment methods because he believed that online methods of payment can steal his money. (Don't misunderstand, that he had a lot of money in his bank account). As a result, he always requests people to pay his bills online and recharge his mobile number. This is how his life is going up. He lost many opportunities because he never opened a Demat account due to his privacy concerns. He thought that the Demat account would breach his privacy. Now, this type of ancient thought only stops him from taking the advantage of the best services that he can have. This stops him from enjoying the facilities. People only lose opportunities by this kind of belief system. They also ignore opportunities by doing this kind of shit. These kinds of people may feel that social media and these kinds of digital platforms are not good for a good person.

Paper Currency

When the first time paper currency was introduced, people refused to accept it as a national currency, and they started to spread rumors against it. People started to rumors that this is a scheme to collect all the gold from them. They don't believe in these paper notes. People started protesting. The government was really worried about this, and they were trying to do every possible solution for it. Somehow, they persuaded the public to accept the paper currency and successfully stopped protests. But people started to speculate on this, they started to accept paper currency at a lower value as per the gold coin. That was a real challenge to deal with these people. The government announced a fine to those people who were involved in such activities. After a long struggle, the government successfully implemented paper currencies. Why didn't I mention any country name in this paragraph? Because it happened in many countries at different times. When their governments introduced paper currencies.

Now, everyone knows that gold has no direct exchange value in the market. It may be legal or illegal subject to the country's law, but it is unofficial everywhere. Nobody can purchase food and other necessary items with the help of gold. No one can say it, please give me a car, I will pay in gold coins. Nobody is going to accept these offers. So always be an early adopter because it is better to adapt to changes early and enjoy the privileges of a first comer. It is worse when it becomes a compulsion to adapt to change or the system forces you to adapt. People who adapt to change easily tend to enjoy it. They can enjoy the journey. The one who doesn't accept it, become the challenges for the system, and they also become losers.

Why this story was important is because this story tells us that people love their opinion towards things, and they don't want to change it easily, but these people always realize their ignorance. We have to choose: either we adapt to change, or we will be forced to adapt to change by the situation.

Never Oppose New Ideas

Change starts with an idea. If you have a personality to oppose every new idea then you may lose the opportunity to start the change. However, anyone else will start the change with the same idea, and you will regret that. New Ideas may offer easy ways to do work, new Ideas can make your work convenient. When someone opposes new Ideas, they unconsciously agree to be pissed off by traditional ideas. Ideas may fail or be successful, but every Idea deserves a try. By opposing new Ideas a person may lose the opportunity to be successful, a person who always opposes new Ideas is creating obstacles in his way. These people rarely get success in their life. Because they assume that they are right in every situation, and they don't need any new ideas and ways to be successful. They repeat the same mistakes for years, which is why they are less likely to achieve success in their life. We can't imagine better results by repeating the same actions. To succeed in life, one needs to understand that people can have new and better ideas that can make you successful. By arguing with people, we can lose the opportunity for something greater. A person who wants to achieve success in life should always be open to new ideas.

Google Chrome,

In the beginning, Google was just a search engine. It was running its business by providing search engine facilities in browsers like Internet Explorer and Mozilla Firefox. Sunder Pichai was concerned that Microsoft will set Bing as the default search engine to its browser. He told this concern to his team manager. He requested his manager to support him to develop Google's web browser. But his manager rejected his Idea. He said to Sunder that your concerns are baseless. After the disappointment from the manager, Sunder talked to Google's CEO Larry Page about his Idea. He impressed Larry Page with his intelligence and futuristic vision. Larry Page gave him an opportunity. And Google started developing its Web browser under the leadership of Sunder Pichai. As Sunder was concerned, Microsoft set Bing as a pre-installed default search engine. Google's existence was at risk because of Microsoft. Microsoft had a clear vision of ruling the internet world through its browser and search engine. Microsoft was aggressive towards its vision. But because of Sunder Pichai Google was also ready to tackle this situation. In 2008 Google launched their Web Browser Chrome where google was the default search engine. We all know the rest of the success story of Google.

Chrome's story clears that new ideas should always be welcomed. Sunder's Idea helped Google become a giant. Your next Idea can change the world, so never oppose new Ideas. Achievers Like Sunder and Larry Page always respect and listen to others' ideas.

Keynotes

A rigid person can never accomplish a big goal in his life.

Be a flexible person.

Adapt changes easily, because nothing is permanent in this materialistic universe.

People who adapt to changes easily take advantage of being first comers.

Never oppose change, change is the universal truth.

Part Two

PREPARE YOURSELF

V
Educate Yourself

Education System

Education is the basis of every achievement. We go to school for education, but schools don't teach us life lessons. Schools do not teach us how to accomplish goals, and how to be successful. Schools only focus on sharpening the memory. They do not have any way to test the skills. Many people who failed in school have achieved massive success in their life.

Because of the lame education system, a person grows up without any knowledge of life. Schools teach subjects in combinations; many of them are irrelevant for students. Schools can't tell the benefit of knowing the history of every politician, they just want to make us read that because that is the syllabus. A person who wants to be a doctor or engineer, what will he do after knowing the history of politicians and movements?

The education system is teaching more irrelevant and useless information that has no relation with the real world. Furthermore, it continues after school. When a person prepares for a job, he has to read the same stuff there.

There are no lessons on how one can achieve goals in his life. The education system is dragging people into the rat race. That is why when asked, 90% of people are unsuccessful in achieving their goals. Schools are providing useless knowledge to students. Where they only learn about places, history, science, and art, but these people are not prepared for life challenges. People can never achieve their goals based on this knowledge.

Only Humans Can Learn From Others

A Donkey falls in a pit, every night when he goes back home (from work) the donkey curses humans for not filling that pit, but he never tried to avoid that pit.

The Dog also fell into the pit Once. He saw a tree nearby that pit and marked that tree as a red flag in his mind. At night whenever he went near that tree he got alerted because he had marked the tree as a red flag in his mind, and he never fell again in that pit because he learned from his mistake.

The Man never fell into that pit. Because he had seen the donkey and dog falling in the pit. So he learned from others' experiences and this is the special quality we humans have.

Only we humans can learn from others' mistakes. This is 2021, and we have machines and technology to assist us. In this century we don't have to fall into a pit just to learn something we can learn from others' mistakes, we can watch case studies on failures. If a person only learns from his own mistakes, he will need to make millions of mistakes. These mistakes only waste time. **"Life's too short to learn everything from your own mistakes"**. It is not necessary to lose something to learn something.

We, humans, have a powerful brain, We have the highest consciousness than other living beings, We are the most beautiful creation of the almighty.

How Humans Became The Wisest Beings

Have you ever thought about how humans became the most powerful and wise beings on planet earth? Because humans can learn from others' mistakes and can transfer knowledge to the next generation through communication skills. So the next generation can learn from our mistakes. This is why we are the most powerful beings on planet earth. Because of communication skills, humans have grown so much. Because of communication skills, humans were able to transfer their knowledge to the next generation.

At the time of evolution, humans learned to communicate and transfer their knowledge to the next generation by communication skills. So they would be less likely to repeat the same mistake. By doing this, the next generation did not die by making the same mistakes. Their next-generation had time to experience new things, to learn something new. They continued the process and transferred their knowledge to the next generation. Every generation was adding their personal experience, as a result, they were sharing more than they got from their ancestors. This addition of experience was increasing the level of knowledge of every next generation. The information and knowledge grew with every generation. This process continued with each generation of humans. They used to receive knowledge from their ancestors and add their personal experience, and then they pass it to the next generation. So their next generation did not need to waste time in learning the same things by their own experience. After some generations, humans collected enough data to survive safely. So they started to explore the world and its secrets. Once they have enough knowledge to survive safely, they start to explore luxuries. Human civilization started creating weapons to rule. They started focusing on inventions of luxury items because they had enough time to think about those things. Human brains started growing. Humans did not have to waste time learning everything from personal experience.

It became human culture to transfer knowledge from one generation to another generation. In this process, humans invented scripts. They started using scripts to transfer their knowledge. After the invention of the script, it became easy to transfer more knowledge to more people in less time. With this invention, knowledge became portable from one place to another place. Spreading the knowledge became easy and convenient, there was no need to travel individually to spread the knowledge.

If humans had not started to transfer knowledge from one generation to another generation, in that case, every generation would have died in the race of survival. If one generation who started to control the fire had not taught another generation the use of fire, then the next generation would die in trying to use the fire. Every generation's lifespan would end in survival. We survived easily because of learning skills because we were able to learn from others' experiences and failures. If the human race had followed the philosophy of learning everything by themselves, then humans would still be dying in the race of survival.

Never Hesitate to Choose Easy

Suppose a brilliant scientist wants to find everything by his own experience, so he works hard to invent the formula of relativity by himself because he wants to learn everything by his life and own experience. And he successfully invents the formula of relativity after 20 years... Is it worth it? No! Not at all because he just wasted his time, he could add value in 20 years with his brilliance. If he had understood the relativity theory from Einstein's work, he could invent many inventions by using existing knowledge. You may be thinking that what a foolish scientist he is or what an irrelevant example it was but, **people who say that they will learn everything from their own experience do the same**. Wise people grow knowledge by using existing knowledge and stupid people learn everything from their mistakes. Choosing easy options and learning from others' mistakes saves time, resources, and money.

People who say that they learn everything from their own experience. They must invent their own languages and scripts. They must learn driving from their own experience?

Life is too short to learn everything from your own experience. There is nothing that has not happened before. So why don't we learn from the past? Why waste time learning everything by own experience?

You don't have to experience those ugly experiences because someone has already experienced them, and he has given them to you. So take it and use your brain to achieve your goals. **Don't waste your time to discover a question's answer that is already answered.**

Learning Attitude

Characters of the story!

The Donkey

Those people who don't learn from their and others' mistakes. They don't want to learn new skills. They all make the same mistakes as everyone did in history. After a certain age, they give the same advice of wisdom that nobody listens to. They do not have any goal to achieve.

Many species of animals may become extinct in the future, but we will have a species of losers in the future.

The Dog

These people believe in learning everything from their own mistakes. They try everything to experience and learn. They do not achieve much in their life because they always use **"try and fail"** methods to learn. By using a try-and-fail method, they waste a lot of time learning little things. That is why they rarely get success in accomplishing their goal. **"Life is too short to learn everything from your own mistakes, learn from others and let them do mistakes"**.

The Man

As we discussed before, humans can learn from others and grow their knowledge. We humans rule the earth because we can learn from others' experiences and mistakes. Humans can learn everything without making mistakes and losses. **By learning from others you can learn to control the fire without burning your hands.**

Find A Guru

To accomplish a goal, we need knowledge and skills. To learn skills, we require a guru. To start a journey of achieving a goal, the journey must start with learning. Knowledge is the real power. A person must have some knowledge before starting anything new. Start with learning practical knowledge.

Many people don't know where to learn, and they just scroll through social platforms, the internet, and start following everyone related to that subject. This is the biggest blunder that one can do to himself. Wrong knowledge can cause huge losses. (I am not saying that free platforms are not teaching you right, there are a lot of good teachers there)

So here I'll tell you some techniques to find a good teacher or other sources of genuine knowledge.

Here are a few steps to find a true Guru and sources.

- First, go to google and search about the established leaders or successful people of your field, who already accomplished what you want to accomplish. Search have they written any book? If yes, then buy those books. Find the best books in your field, order them, and read them all.
- Make notes on that book.
- Watch all interviews of successful people in your field.
- Read and watch their biographies.
- Attend seminars related to your field.

- If you want to learn from social platforms, pick 10 videos or articles from a free educator. Then verify the information given by that source, from various other sources, and if his information is proven correct in your due diligence and cross-check then you can learn from him.

How To Find a Good Teacher?

In 2014, I decided to learn about money, the stock market, and entrepreneurship. I faced a huge problem because everyone was selling their courses there. I didn't know anything about them. I got meaningless answers as I asked about their achievements.

The first one answered that I have studied at the top universities in the country. The second 10000 people have subscribed to my course. Isn't it enough to introduce myself? Third, I have been doing this work for 30 years.

No one was able to tell their achievements in the stock market and entrepreneurship. I simply asked them What will I do with their experience? You seem to be good sellers because you are selling courses? I am not here to learn to sell, I will feel cheated if I book losses in the stock market after learning from you. In the end, they all got offended.

Recently I purchased a course on entrepreneurship by Ankur Warikoo. Ankur Warikoo has achieved business success. He is a well-known entrepreneur. What can be better than this if successful entrepreneurs teach us as our teachers. This is the best combination that one can have.

If someone is teaching business, then search for his achievements. He could be a fake teacher just to earn money. If he earns money only by selling courses. This is the first sign of a fake teacher. If he doesn't have achieved anything in that field, then how can he teach you? He will just teach you theoretical materials. That you can learn from anywhere for free. How can you learn to ride a bike from a person who doesn't ride himself?

A person who wants to learn practical knowledge like business needs to learn from a real guru like Dr. Vivek Bindra. You should always learn these kinds of skills from legends. He is a legend who fits best for example. Now, which qualities make Dr. Vivek Bindra a legend in the business world.

- Dr. Vivek Bindra has built his own super successful business empire.
- Dr. Vivek Bindra's ethics are very high. It can be seen in his free videos as Asia's no1 business couch gives free leadership seminars on YouTube.
- Provides special discounts to women to empower them.
- Provides special discounts to students because he knows students don't have a high budget.
- Dr. Vivek Bindra offers the most affordable programs.
- He collaborates with the most successful entrepreneurs, and he brings them to teach his students.

Price and value matters

A person should always compare price differences before purchasing the course. A learner should do due diligence before subscribing to a course online or offline. These questions can help one in the due diligence of a course.

- Who is the educator?
- Educator's accomplishments?
- Can you learn it for free from somewhere else?
- If you are learning it for free then you have to crosscheck facts, at least you should crosscheck every fact three times. For Example, if you are watching free videos related to the stock market (discounted cash flow) then you should cross-check video data on Investopedia and Zerodha Pulse. Many people can give you wrong information related to the subject.

- Always compare the price of courses. Many courses have cheap and reliable substitutes.
- Search on Google about your course educator. Add scam or fraud with his name on Google, Google will show you all controversies related to him. It will help you to make informed decisions.
- If someone has a mobile application then, see its rating and read its reviews.

Many courses offer only basic information. Like some excel courses, you can learn it for free from social platforms like YouTube. If your extra effort can save you money, then you should save money.

Keynotes

- Right education is very important to accomplish goals
- Humans can also learn from other people's mistakes.
- Life is too short to learn everything from your own mistakes
- Always learn from an achiever guru.
- Don't subscribe to anything without due diligence.
- Avoid a guru whose only achievement is selling courses.

VI
Your Hero

Your life is the result of your choices. The concept of heroes is important. We all had heroes when we were children, Millennials heroes were Superman, Spider-Man, X-Man, Iron Man, etc. We all wanted to be like them in our childhood but as we grew up we understood that these are only fictional heroes, they don't have any relation with reality. They only exist in comics.

We human beings always try to become what we follow. As Shree Krishna Says in Shreemad Bhagwad Geeta ***"Followers do the same as the leader"***. Why choose, Singers and actors as heroes? They are good actors and singers but not heroes. They may have good acting skills, but it doesn't mean that they are heroes. They can only teach us acting skills. If you want to be an actor then you should follow them, they are your heroes. There is no other reason to call them heroes and follow them. I have seen many people who dedicated their lives to a movie. I call them Gaga. They love to follow an actor/actress, and they dwell in the character of that actor. It starts with copying their hairstyle, and then it grows one step ahead, and then they start making tattoos of that actor, and it goes on and on.

Heroes build a nation. If a nation has good, honest, and brave heroes, then the nation will have brave and honest citizens.

India's every citizen is a motherland lover. Indian citizens are always ready to sacrifice their lives for the motherland. It's something that no one can remove from an Indian's heart. Why are all Indians nationalist? Because they are grown up by listening to the stories of patriotism of Netaji Subhash Chandra Bose, Gandhi, Ashfaq Ullah Khan, and Bhagat Singh. That's why every Indian has a patriotic sentiment.

India vs Pakistan Cricket

Now, when we talk about India, India v/s Pakistan cricket match comes to mind. In the modern age, both countries have cricket teams, where Pakistan has always good bowlers and India has maximum good Batsmen. This is because in Pakistan their early cricketers were good bowlers, and they created an Impact. On the other hand, India's early cricketers were good batsmen and they also created an impact. That's why Indian cricket lovers have batsman heroes they follow them with a die heart and India has maximum good batsmen. Where Pakistani cricket lovers have bowler heroes, and it reflects at the playground.

How To Find the Perfect Hero?

How to find a perfect hero for you? Who can be your hero? How can your hero help to make you successful?

Now the first thing to understand is that your hero must be a positive character, he must have a positive image in society. Like a successful entrepreneur, a successful cricketer, a successful politician, a successful scientist, or a successful administrator(Like RBI governor or any successful administrator. If you want to become an IAS officer, then your known IAS officer could be your hero. If you want to become part of an intelligence agency, then Mr. Ajit Dovel can be your hero. Your hero should be a person that matches your ambition). A hero who has accomplished what you want to accomplish. **"Shree Krishna says a person becomes what he focuses on"**. So your hero should be already there where you want to be. He must be an achiever, he must have accomplished his goals.

Synergy

Many people choose negative heroes in their life. It became fashionable to choose a hippie hero in modern society. People choose drug-addicted people as their heroes. Dreadlock hairstyles became very famous these days because of those hippie singers. These days, people have developed a mindset that negative characters are cool. People feel very proud to say that I drank 2 or 3 bottles of liquor or used drugs to enjoy. They wear skeleton design T-Shirts and think that is cool. They don't know that these kinds of interests can make you depressed at the mental level.

These things are not cool, being a hippie is not cool, one should behave politely. A person should be polite. A hippie look is not a funky look. The definition of hippies, hippies(formed in 1960) is uncivilized people who often stay beside the road do sex on the roadside, associated with a subculture involving a rejection of conventional values and the taking of hallucinogenic drugs. They usually keep long hair, tattooed bodies, and don't bathe for many days or years, always using abusive words. (Please don't get me wrong, I am not against long hair and tattooed bodies and I didn't mean that every person who has a tattooed body or long hair is a hippie). I want to say to those people who intentionally or unintentionally follow a hippie by thinking that hippie is cool or trendy. I want to tell them that you don't have to become a hippie to be cool. A classy and good-looking man with clean hair is cool. The biggest thing is that it builds ethics.

Choose A Positive Hero

Always choose a positive hero in your life. **Because you have to follow him and to follow him you need synergy**. First, you must look for your qualities and passion, then you should try to match them with a perfect hero. Suppose, you have good business skills, then Bill Gates and other entrepreneurs are best suitable heros. If you are good at singing, then Akon or any other singer could be suitable here. But if you have good entrepreneurial skills, and you are following an actor, then you are on the wrong plane that can crash your life. Being a fan is okay! But you should not see him or her as your hero. **"Your hero should be a person who has already achieved the goal that you want to achieve".**

Nowadays, it has become a fashion to criticize entrepreneurs. The middle class is blaming them for their poorness. The Middle Class is blaming them that they are close to the government and that's why they are rich. They are entrepreneurs. They should be close to the government in case we want to grow our nation. Without cooperation, countries, entrepreneurs constantly grow. Entrepreneurs create jobs. Entrepreneurs help to grow a country, they contribute to the nation's GDP. Most of the billionaires are big philanthropists, they help people, they donate a lot of money. In COVID-19 situations, many entrepreneurs donated thousands of crores. On the other hand, you'll hardly find a politician who has donated a penny. So why not see entrepreneurs as heroes? Entrepreneurs are the best suitable heroes to those who want to be rich.

Never Hesitate Copy your Hero

Try to think as your hero thinks. Imagine him in your situation then think what he would do if he were at your place, do that. Copy his good habits, study him and try to understand his ways of thinking. Read about him and watch his interviews if you know the person personally, then try to spend more time with him to know more about him. Do what he would do if he were at your place. This is the best and easiest way to be successful in life for a person who wants easy solutions to every problem. Copying heroes is a proven way to get the best results. Because here you don't need to invent a new system, you don't need to work hard on thinking about a new system. You don't need to come up with an extraordinary idea. You don't have to hassle and try new experiments. Risk and investment are also low. **Copying a successful person is less costly and the easiest way to become a successful person.** Your hero worked hard and designed a system, and you just have to copy him to be successful.

On planet earth, we have some laws for everything. If you throw a stone in the air, then it will come back because of gravity. If you heat water to 100 degrees Celsius then it will boil. Same if you follow the path of successful people, your chances of becoming successful are very high. **"Success is a destination where you can reach by following successful people's footprints".** It is easy because you know the path. You can see ahead because your hero is already there. You know your next step.

Copying someone is not a bad thing if it can make you successful in your life. There is nothing unethical in copying your hero, you can admit that you copied your hero. It is as simple as learning and implementing. Show smartness, learn from others, and implement it in your life.

Secret Of Monks' Success

Let's talk about the monks because they are on the way to ultimate success. They are on the way to salvation. They are on the way to achieving ultimate success, they are on the way to achieving the spiritual goal. So what do they do exactly? They simply copy the path of their spiritual master. For example, **every Buddhist monk doesn't discover new ways of salvation; he simply follows Buddha's way. Monks copy every teaching of the Buddha and "it works".** As I mentioned before, this earth has some laws that work in the same way for everyone on this planet. If Buddha discovered a way of salvation and got salvation by that. Then it has become a proven way of salvation. It is certain that whoever follows his path honestly, definitely gets salvation, he also reaches where Buddha reached. (Similarly, all religions people follow their spiritual leaders or prophets' way to get salvation). We humans believe that salvation is the ultimate success and nothing is more valuable than salvation. So it becomes more clear here. When we can successfully achieve our spiritual goal by copying our spiritual leader, then obviously we can achieve materialistic goals by following materialistic achievers.

By copying, risk reduces uncertainty. We could be comfortable with the results by copying the path because we can see him as our future.

If you are feeling offended because you don't copy anyone, you invent your new ways of doing everything, it is also fine. For that, you must be hard working. You must have money in your bank account. We could never have reached here without the help of people who invent new. We would never have Microsoft if Bill Gates hadn't tried something new, We would never have Apple if Steve Jobs wouldn't be a hard worker (Both have different ethics of business no one copied another one).

Keynotes

- Your hero should be an achiever, a person who already has achieved goals that you want to achieve in your life.
- If you don't want to go through a long process, then don't hesitate to copy your hero, don't hesitate to follow his way and go through his way.

VII
You Must Deserve It

Chase success because you need it, it doesn't care about you. Many people try new things or work in new programs to be successful. For example, many people start a startup and their first startup fails. Then they start their next startup and their next startup also fails, so they try it 4 to 5 times. After that, they feel pity and they quit. They show like they are now upset with success because success didn't touch their toes after their 5 tries. They behave like saying; hey success! I was the best person who deserves you. I was the perfect person but you! Egoistic success broke my heart, and now I don't care about you. After showing this attitude, people think that success is going to run after them and say oh! Sorry Prince I was waiting for you, I am all yours, I was unable to hear you cry. Now please take me with you, I am your biggest fan, you are my hero. This is like a fairy tale, but broken people behave like this. This attitude never lets you be successful.

Many people choose God to do it, they think that God is only there to serve a person who cries for every little wish. These people believe that God will serve them once they are upset with him. If their wishes don't get fulfilled, then they become atheists. They say, I no longer believe in God because he is unfair to me. I believed in God, but he didn't give me what I wanted. These people should be atheists because they stopped trying and lost their self-confidence.

They don't even believe in themselves then how they can believe in god. (God is with those people who never accept failure, who do work until the success)

Success is not your girlfriend who will try to save her relationship with you. Success will not run after you if you are upset with it. **Success doesn't care about your mood, it doesn't care about your broken heart**. I will never miss you. Success will not say that, oh! I am missing him. He was the best person for me, and he tried so hard for me. Let's go get him. Success never feels guilty of any person.

Success only cares about how much you are trying to get it, how much you love success. If you stop trying new ways to get success, then it forgets you. Success loves a dedicated person. Success is yours if you chase it until you have it.

Billionaire Steve Jobs said in his speech, "If you say daily that this is your last day of life, you will be right one day. Steve Jobs explained this principle in a single line. The message is clear that if you try every day to accomplish a goal, then definitely you will accomplish that goal.

Persistence

Persistence is the quality of continuing steadily despite problems or difficulties. It is one of the qualities of high achievers. The longer you stay committed to a task or goal, the more likely something good will happen for you. And believe me- the Universe will test your commitment to your goal. You develop yourself and learn new lessons, you face challenges and obstacles, but the payoff comes when you refuse to give up. Have you heard that anything worth having is worth working for? It's true. Some of my most difficult situations preceded tremendous breakthroughs. There are tons of examples of underdogs, heroes, who persisted, met, or even exceeded their goals.

Jack Ma

Jack Ma is an appropriate example of persistence. Jack Ma was not a good student. "Jack Ma failed a key primary school test two times. He failed the middle school test three times, he failed the college entrance exam two times. Jack Ma scored 1 out of 120 points on the math portion of his college entrance exam. And it wasn't because he didn't have time to prepare. This was because Jack Ma struggles with mathematics. Furthermore, Jack Ma was rejected from Harvard 10 times.

After graduating from college, he applied to 30 different jobs and was subsequently rejected by all of them. He was the only interviewee (out of 24) rejected by KFC. Out of 24 KFC applicants in his pool, 23 were hired. Jack Ma was the only one to be rejected. He attributes this largely to his lack of good looks and short stature. Jack Ma is the paradigm of persistence.

Here are more examples of persistence.

- Tim Ferriss sent his breakthrough New York Times bestselling book 4-Hour Workweek to 25 publishers before one finally accepted it.
- Henry Ford's early businesses failed and left him broke 5 times before he founded Ford Motor Company.
- Walt Disney went bankrupt after failing at several businesses. He was even fired from a newspaper for lacking imagination and good ideas. WALT DISNEY or lack of imagination, isn't it funny?
- Stephen R. Covey, the author of The Seven Habits of Highly Effective People, created one of the largest leadership development companies in the world. Before the company was worth $160 million, the company endured 11 straight years of negative cash flow.
- Before Sylvester Stallone was a famous writer and actor, he was rejected by over 600 casting agents and was unable to sell his

first 8 screenplays.

- Albert Einstein was thought to be mentally handicapped before changing the face of modern physics and winning the Nobel Prize.
- Lucille Ball was regarded as a failed actress before she won 4 Emmys and the Lifetime Achievement Award from the Kennedy Center Honors.
- Dr. Seuss's first book was rejected by 27 publishers before it was accepted.
- American author Jack London received 600 rejections before his first story was accepted. That is some thick skin!
- Vincent van Gogh sold only one painting in his lifetime, though today, his works are priceless.
- Michael Jordan was cut from his high school basketball team for not being good enough.
- It took Thomas Edison 1,000 attempts before inventing the light bulb. His teachers also told him growing up that he was too stupid to learn anything.

Conclusion

There are no failures in life, only those who quit before success. **The formula for success is trying until you succeed**. If you give up during the struggle, you will never experience victory.

Deserve It

You must understand the fact that people only get what they deserve. If someone gets a lot of wealth in inheritance without deserving it, then he doesn't stay wealthy. We have many examples in history where people were unable to keep inherited wealth. If someone deserves a lot of wealth, but he doesn't have it, then soon he will have it. This is the universal law. This universe is fair with everyone. Many people may relate it with the law of karma. Because your Karma decides your worth. Karma is fair with everyone. It is the same as the law of gravity: if a rich person throws a stone towards the sky, then it falls back on earth due to gravity. Similarly, if a poor person throws the stone towards the sky then it also falls back on the earth. It doesn't matter who is throwing the stone.

So you must become a deserving person of your goals. It doesn't matter who you are, male or female, child or adult, if you deserve your goal you will achieve it. If you want to become a billionaire, then you must deserve it. You must prove that you deserve it. You must learn everything about being a billionaire. You must have similar knowledge as billionaires have.

This universe always gives you what you deserve. **"Do your best karma, so karma can do best to you".** The law of karma is undeniable. **If someone says that this law doesn't work on him, then first he must prove that the law of gravity doesn't work on him.** Be a deserving person of success, and success will come to you. If you don't do karma to change your life, then karma will also do nothing for you to change your life. Work on yourself. Undoubtedly you will get what you deserve.

A person who fights with everyone only gets fights back. A person who abuses everyone only gets abused back, because that is what he deserves.

Be a great man

You have to be a great man to be successful in life. You have to implement each lesson of this book. Information can't make you successful, only implementations can. A great man never quits, never loses hope. For a great man, there is only one end that is a success. Everyone faces difficulties in life, and many quit and spread rumors of failure. They spread rumors that nothing works and luck is the only factor that is required for life. They spread rumors that they have tried every way, but nothing works. But they are just quitters. Don't listen to those people, they are just good examples of failures and quitters. **You can learn from them too, but the lesson is**

all about don'ts. You don't have to follow their advice, don't have to do what they did, and don't have to experience like them. A big no for everything.

Dedication

Motivation is important, but only motivation can't make you successful in life. Motivation needs dedication. Success formula is: **Motivation+dedication = success.**

People never dedicate themselves to a goal. Many times people get motivated but when it comes to doing something towards a goal they avoid doing work. People believe that they deserve every best thing, but they fail to prove it.

Believing that you deserve it is the first step. You need to clear it in mind that it is 80% about the mindset and 20% skills. So first, believe that you deserve it. This belief gives you the energy to acquire the required skills. (This 80% will give you the energy to acquire 20% skills). **The second step is proving that you deserve it.** To prove that you deserve it, you need to be dedicated to your goal. You need to do everything that can be done to achieve a goal.

Meditation gives visible results with dedication. Only visualizing good things is not called dedication. Dedication is when you give your time to a goal when you do more than your capacity. When you don't get stuck in your limits. **Dedication is When you don't waste time feeling disappointed, because your goal is much bigger than disappointments.**

A person who is not dedicated to his goal can never achieve his goals. Some people want to become billionaires, but they don't want to read a few books to learn something. They believe that they deserve and can achieve their goal, but they never take appropriate actions, they never prove it. They only want the fruit, but they never want to plant a tree.

Never Regret

Never regret any mistake because regret stops you from taking further action. **Not taking any decision is the worst decision.** A person who regrets a lot can see fewer opportunities as compared to a positive person. Regret is dangerous to your mental health. Never feel guilty about any mistake. Remember you have to be a great man to be successful in life and a great man never regrets.

What regret has to offer you? Depression? Anxiety? When does regret come? Regret can never delete your mistake, then why do you regret it? (Many people regret at the time of the death of their beloved one. But regret can't bring back a dead person). A wise man never regrets because regret stops a person from growing. Regret is an obstacle in the way of achieving goals in life. **Regret leads to dissatisfaction, and dissatisfaction fills a person's mind with sadness. Furthermore, sadness leads to anger, and anger steals a person's wisdom and ability to think wisely and do good.** Regret is the start of the downfall. This is why great achievers never regret; rather, they learn from mistakes and improve themselves. **Invest time in improving yourself instead of regretting it. Don't revise your mistakes. Learn lessons and implement them in your life.**

Never complain

A beggar was begging for money on the roadside. A woman begged him for 5 cents. Beggar immediately replied, "What will I do with these 5 cents? It can't even buy a packet of bread. You **MISER**, you should give me more". The woman felt ashamed and regretted giving him 5 cents. She decided that she will never beg that beggar again. Some people do this with the universe. When a person achieves a little success, he immediately says that I needed more, but you gave me less. The universe also regrets giving him. And try to not give him anything again. So an achiever never complains about his circumstances and his situation.

Complaints shift you "little to nothing", it shifts focus from solution to the problem. Complaints just increase the level of your dissatisfaction. So never waste your energy in complaining, so you can find a solution to every issue. Forget about the complaints. Train your mind to find solutions. Don't act like a beggar. Don't be inconsiderate. Complaints give a message to this universe that you are not satisfied with the little blessing of this universe. As a result, the universe perceives it as a failed investment in you, and it never likes to invest again in you. Universal consciousness is the giver, and you are the receiver. If the receiver is not happy after receiving a little, then this universe does not like to give him more. A person who focuses on less. The output will be less. His mind's programming will be for less only. Your mind is like soil. It doesn't care what you sow in it, it grows everything in the same. Complain Only if you want more complaints in your life, complaint only if you want to become a helpless person in your life.

Gratitude

Never feel satisfied with your work, it will motivate you to do more work, always desire to achieve more. If your outcome is less than your work then your next outcome will be more than your work, gratitude has an effect of compounding. If you complain about your first outcome, then you will not have a better outcome. It is not only about the power of positive thinking. It also has a mental aspect. A complaining person's mind develops a habit of complaining. The mind starts seeking problems in every solution.

So that is why a person must have gratitude to achieve more because gratitude has two ways to give you more. One is the way where gratitude towards the universe serves you more. Second, gratitude keeps your mind calm. It is not a hidden fact that a calm mind can generate better ideas to be successful. Achievers show gratitude towards every little achievement.

Thank the universe if you achieve something and if you fail to achieve then thank the universe for the next time in advance. The universe will return your thanks by fulfilling your wishes.

It is never late

A person should start his success journey as soon as possible, but it is never late. It doesn't matter at which time you start your journey because everyone has some priorities and some obligations. Where many people do not have clarity about their life goals, so they start their journey late. But always remember it is never late. Ray Kroc and Colonel Sanders started their journey at the age of 53 and 72 respectively. They didn't feel late to start a startup. They did what they wanted in their life. They didn't feel old until they achieved their goal. You have to do the same, you just have to believe in yourself. You always have to be ready to start every time and at every age.

No one remembers his previous life. No one has the afterlife experience to share. The world only remembers people who have done great works in this life. Whenever you think that it is too late, always ask one question to yourself: **when people will remember me after my death, then how do I want to be remembered?** Do you want to be remembered as a loser or as an achiever? **"Just imagine about your funeral, can anybody say that you were not a great person because you achieved success after so many failed attempts, or you were not great because you started your journey late"**.

The Almighty God has created us. He has a great purpose for every child. I believe that nobody fails in this universe because God has an abundance of success for everyone. There is no existence of failure in this universe. There are only two types of people, achievers, and quitters. Nobody would know about Thomas Alva Edison if he had quieted after the 9998 failure. Failures are just unsuccessful attempts of success. Only losers accept failure by quitting; winners never accept failure; they don't accept anything less than success. You must believe in your dream, you must believe that your goal is easy to achieve. There is no space for failure words in the achiever's dictionary. Only quitter defines unsuccessful attempts as a failure.

When we learn to ride a bicycle, we fall many times. It can happen 1000 times, but nobody considers it a failure. Nobody says that yesterday he failed to ride a bicycle, and can never ride a bicycle. We all show an attitude that it was the process of learning. But when it comes to achieving a goal, why don't people show the same attitude, as they show at the riding time?

Keynotes

- You must deserve what you want in your life.
- Chase success because you need success.
- Be a deserving guy, learn everything that is required to be what you want to be.
- Persist until you make it happen in your life, there are no back doors.
- Dedicate yourself to your goal.
- Never regret any failure because regret does not let you learn from the failure.
- Understand people and make good relations with them.
- Never complain about the less you have because complaints give you nothing from less.
- It's never too late to be successful in life.
- Only success matters, in the end, nobody cares when you started and how many times you failed. People only talk about your success.
- **Nobody cares about the loser's struggle.**

VIII
Achieve Goals

Clarity In Goals

Have you ever set a goal that you never achieved? There may be many, ever asked why? Do you know many failed people are one step away from their goals?

Why do average people fail to achieve their goals in life? In their 20s everyone wants to be rich, but in 35 they only want to earn money just to fulfill their family's needs.

Many people have miss conceptions about goals. They think buying a new mobile phone or car is their goal. But these are only desires and needs. You should have a goal that can add value to your life.

How to become clear about your goal? The biggest question arrives: what should a person do, who has many so-called goals? How to get clarity about goals and how to prioritize the goal?

- If your goal is adding value in life.
- A goal that meets all your needs. Which could be a one-stop solution for many wishes. (If you think that buying a house is your goal, then understand that after buying a house, you will desire to buy a big house and luxury items. Your goal can be

wealth if you have these kinds of needs. Being wealthy is the one-stop solution for you. It will fulfill all your wishes)
- It should define yourself. It should make you happy. It should change your life in a positive direction.
- **It should create a lifetime impact.**

Your goal should be clear, your time is limited. You don't have to go for small satisfactions. Don't waste your energy chasing your desires. Invest your time to chase a goal, not a desire.

Desires v/s Goals

Most people are confused between goals and desires. People call goals to their desires. As we have discussed before, one should not get confused about desires vs goals. Desires give temporary satisfaction and goals give you long-lasting satisfaction. Suppose you have a desire to pass your college in 90%, but you got only 70%. What will you do in this situation? Will you go to college again to get 90%, or will you sacrifice it? You have only 2 options: either go to college again or you may sacrifice it, and move further. In this example you can clearly understand that getting good marks was not your goal, it was a desire or need, but getting a degree was your goal. You will go to college again if you don't get the degree.

A goal is different from a desire. You do not feel satisfied in life If you don't achieve it. You feel bad every time, you feel incomplete without accomplishing your goal. Your inner self fights with you to achieve your goal. It completes your identity, it reflects your personality. It is part of your personality.

So it becomes important to understand the difference between desire v/s goal. So that you don't chase desires in the name of the goal, don't waste energy in running after your desires. Rather, invest your energy in chasing goals. Goals make you successful, not desires, desires bind you.

A desire may bring regret in your life after fulfilling it. You may have heard people who say that their goal is buying a car for the year. Later they regret buying a car because they feel trapped in the trap of EMI. It becomes their need to work for the EMI, whether they like it or not. That is why I said that desire binds us. That is why clarity is essential.

Be a goal-oriented person, not desire-oriented. A child can be desire-oriented, but a man must be goal-oriented.

Focus

Once, Bill Gates and Warren Buffett were requested to explain the secret of their success in a single word. Both were in separate rooms. A white paper and pen had been given to them. They both wrote "focus" on the white paper as their answer. The importance of focus can be understood from the answers of these two legends.

"The main reasons for failure is lack of focus and wrong focus"

Less Focused Person

A person who does not have focus can never accomplish any goal. On the other hand, a less focused person tries things for a couple of days and doesn't complete them. A less focused person can never use his 100% abilities to achieve a goal. So it is necessary to be focused, and control on the mind is necessary to be focused. Where lack of focus is a product of distractions, uncontrolled mind, and desires. Fickleness is the nature of the mind; you have to control it to be focused. So to control your mind, you just have to stop yourself dwelling in your mind's fickleness. Your mind may have many thoughts of fickleness. You have to let them come and go out, don't dwell in them. Focus only on your one goal. **It is impossible to stop the mind's fickleness, but it is possible to not dwell on them.** This is the simplest way to deal with the mind's fickleness. This is the simplest way to be focused.

Person Who Focus On desires

If a person focuses on a wrong, then definitely he is going to achieve wrong things in his life. A person may have great focus, but what if his focus is on desires? Or a person whose only focus is on playing video games and impressing girls. What can he achieve in his life? He will achieve what he is focusing on, but definitely, he is going to regret it. So you need to focus on the right things to succeed.

Focus On One Big Goal

Everyone should have one big goal in life. It can be called a life goal. This goal should be the definition of life. A person should grow his personality according to this goal. A person should choose his heroes according to this goal, as we discussed in our previous chapters.

A big goal can be accomplished in many steps. This goal can be divided into many parts. You can have many ways to achieve a goal. Successful people have only one goal at a time. That is why their focus is equal to laser-sharp. They put all their energy into that goal.

You may have seen archers when they aim at a dot, they only focus on that dot. That is how they successfully target the Aim. An archer needs a lot of focus to successfully target the Aim. A distracted archer can never target successfully. People who have many goals at a single time. They try to aim in multiple directions with a single arrow. They are always confused about where to target first. They don't know where to focus first. Many people try to achieve many goals at a single time, and that's why they always fail. They never accomplish their goal. A goal can be achieved in multiple ways, but the goal should be one at a time. Prioritize your one goal and forget about other goals and desires. Choose a goal that can finish the need of achieving other goals. Ask yourself what is that one goal, where after accomplishing that, other goals will be unnecessary. Focus 100% on that goal.

Be Secretive

There are two types of people, One openly announces their goals. Announcers tell their plans and future expectations to everyone. They have got a habit of sharing everything before taking any action. There are many disadvantages of telling your goal to people. People try to demotivate you. People try to limit you.

Second secretive, who keeps their plans and next move secret. These people don't believe in announcing their goals; they like to show results. Secretive people keep their goals secret from everyone and take action secretly. They are underdogs. These people surprise other people with their success.

Psychologists have found that, by telling your goal, you are less likely to accomplish it. By giving voice to your goal, you feel like you've taken a huge step forward. Unfortunately, this feeling—called "social reality" by psychologists—is just that: a feeling. You haven't accomplished anything yet. Saying your goal out loud widens the gap between what you intend to do and what you do. It disembodied the goal from your actions. On the other hand, by keeping your goals secret, you maintain that sense of urgency and drive to keep moving forward. You feel like there's still a lot of work to be done, and you double down on self-discipline and control. You make plans, create to-do lists, and take action. With no one aware of your intent, your intention-behavior gap remains small—exactly where you want it. So you must be secretive to accomplish your goal easily.

Why Do People Fail?

Over expectations

Sometimes the problem is not with goals or not with mindset. The actual issue is our expectations. We take one step and start dreaming of ourselves at the top of Everest. **"One step will not take you to the peak of Everest, but many steps will"**

Many people expect too much from each action, they expect that this action must accomplish their goal. If it doesn't, then they forget their goals. A goal can never be achieved with this attitude. When we expect too much from a single action, we overload our actions with our expectations, we pressurize our actions. It doesn't let us work properly. We create a situation where we can't focus on our actions because of pressure.

Over expectations create attachment towards work. Attachment doesn't let us forget the efforts and the feeling. The person feels awful if it doesn't give desired results. Attachment towards work makes us feel like a broken heart in love. An attached person rarely tries again. Over-expectation leads to huge disappointment. We have the power of doing work and staying positive, that is what Lord Krishna says in Geeta **"do your work without any attachment"**.

The outcome is a natural process, don't think too much about it. Do your work without attachment, you will receive what you deserve. Sometimes results can be unfavorable because of some mistakes. But if we work without attachment, then next time the result will be better than work. So achievers never stress much about the outcome, they don't care about the single outcome, they work until the accomplishment of the goal.

Inconsistency

We must take the second action as soon as possible if the first action fails. If a person consistently takes action to achieve his goal, he achieves his goal. We must try thousands of ways to achieve our goal. If we get 0.10% near to our goal from every action, then a thousand ways will help us 100% to accomplish our goal 100%.

Suppose you are not good at balancing on a rope, what are your chances to cross the 10 meters long rope? Ans is one in a thousand. You have to do it exactly the same, try to cross it a thousand times. **Focus on one goal but try many ways to accomplish it, do everything to accomplish it. Focus on the goal, not on the way.**

"You only need one successful experiment in your life to achieve your goal". You should try it until you make it happen.

You should forget your efforts and failures as Monday's lunch, only learnings should be remembered. Only keep goals in your mind, not your efforts. **"Charge yourself again and run until you achieve the goal. Try so many times, so many ways, so badly that success becomes obvious"**.

The only ending is a happy ending; there is no bad ending in real life.

A person should never assume that it was their last chance. **If you believe that your goal should be achieved in a single attempt, it means you don't have a goal.** You were only speculating on desires. A goal deserves more than a thousand attempts. Never hesitate to try again and again to achieve your goal. Goals may take time to accomplish, but definitely, they will be accomplished.

Not Putting Enough Efforts

Many people do not put their full efforts to achieve their goals. **Goals are not part-time jobs where you don't put your 100% effort.** A goal does not give you a salary, it gives you rewards. A person must give his 100% to accomplish his goal. A person must work beyond his limits to accomplish his goals. Achievers put all of their energy into their goals. Whenever they do something to achieve their goal, they work like wartime. They do every possible way to achieve their goal. They do not hesitate to take favors from others to achieve their goal. **Once a goal has been set it means it has to be achieved in every situation, there is no backdoor to escape. There is only one choice; that is a success, there are no other options.** I challenge you, if you think like this, you will accomplish your every goal. Just develop an attitude that the only end of starting a race is success. Make it your life's purpose. Live for it. Do everything for it. Assume that your life will be nothing without achieving this goal. Keep this goal in mind every time. Prepare yourself mentally and physically. Hustle for it.

Not Taking Risks

There are mainly two types of risks." Necessary and unnecessary risk"

Necessary Risk:

Either one can be the safest person or can be a successful person. Everyone has to take the necessary risks to achieve their goals. Like investment decisions; investments in securities for a higher return. Whenever a person invests in education, he takes risks on time, resources, and money. Whenever a boy asks his best friend for a relationship, he takes risks. So, risks are important to be successful in life. But it's important to understand where to take risks and where to play it safe. First, you need to ask yourself" Is it worth taking the risk? Is it necessary to take risks? If it's necessary, then it should be a calculated risk.

Unnecessary Risk

There is a long list of people who take unnecessary risks. Unnecessary risk can be defined in a single line. **Not using easily available options and wasting time and resources, just to satisfy the ego, is called unnecessary risk.**

"You don't need to invent a plane again just to travel from America to Canada"

Some people aggressively follow the philosophy of taking risks, but they forget to analyze the category of risk like, they take risk in every situation without analyzing it. It is the same as saying **"I cross the river by lifting on the rope and don't take the bridge to cross the river because I am a risk-taker"**.

Everyone should avoid unnecessary risks. Everyone starts their journey to success with limited resources, not everyone has a lot of money to try everything, but everyone can calculate the risk. A person should only take calculated risks. Now understand the calculated risk. Calculated risk is something where you calculate the maximum loss side, and you can live a good life after that loss.

Lack Of Willpower

Motivation is important to set big goals in life. It gives the energy to do great work in life. It can help you to set a big goal in life. Motivation helps you to see your hidden potential. But motivation alone is not enough to achieve goals.

Motivation doesn't work without willpower. You need massive willpower to stay motivated. A disappointed person can never have willpower as a result, motivation doesn't work on him.

You may have realized that motivation energy comes down after some days of watching a motivational video or attending a motivational seminar. Have you ever thought, Why does it happen? The answer is that motivation doesn't work without willpower. People feel very high in the ongoing seminar. They feel energyless after seminars.

Willpower comes from achievement. The size of the achievements doesn't matter. The subconscious mind registers it as an achievement, not by size, achievements are only achievements for the brain, these achievements start to develop willpower in the mind.

These achievements can be small; you can start it by winning small games in your group. It is all about developing your higher willpower, and this willpower helps you to stay motivated to do work and create a winning attitude. You need to be an achiever and can start with achieving small things.

Try Everything To Achieve Your Goal

I don't understand why people save plan B for the latter. It means they believe that their first plan is going to fail. Why don't they work simultaneously on both plans?

You should work on as many plans as you can do to reach your goal. If you work only on a single plan, then you may lose the opportunity of another plan. You may lose the advantage of being the first comer. **There is nothing wrong if you have a plan to scale your success, but it is wrong not giving a chance to all of your plans.** You can focus mainly on a single plan, but simultaneously you must start your other plans on a small scale. It is not about distracting from the main goal. The goal remains the same, but try many ways to achieve it. Time is a big issue if you only work on one plan. I am not saying that you should try multitasking. **"Focusing on two goals is multitasking".** But if you are working on a single goal and choose two ways to achieve it then it is not multitasking, it is called smart working. If you work on two plans together, then you are using your time more efficiently. It will pay you more efficiently.

Elon Musk runs his many companies simultaneously. Google operates multiple businesses simultaneously. These are the ways to rapidly achieve a goal. One should focus his whole energy on a single goal, but he should try every possible way to achieve it.

You must execute all your plans without wasting time. It doesn't matter how many plans you have. You must execute all of your plans, for that you should leverage people. Do not attach with a single plan, don't be rigid, try everything that you can to be successful. You can prioritize your plans, for example, you can give your 90% time to a single plan and 10% time for the rest of the plans.

Focus is important but does not focus on the way, focus on the goal. Here we have divided plans into 4 categories.

1. RISKY LESS REWARDING
2. SAFE, LESS REWARDING
3. RISKY MORE REWARDING
4. SAFE REWARDING

Here we have 4 categories of plans. First, we have to categorize plans into these four categories.

If your combination is "Risky, more rewarding plus safe and rewarding" then give your 30% to more rewarding and risky. And give 70% time and resources to the safe and rewarding plan.

If your combination is "risky but less rewarding plus safe rewarding" then give your 5% time and resources to risky and less rewarding. And give 95% to your rewarding and safe plan.

If your plan combination is "safe rewarding plus safe less rewarding" then give your 90% to your safe rewarding and 10% to safe, less rewarding.

Always remember in every situation you have to keep a "SAFE, REWARDING" plan in your combination where you can rely on it.

Keynotes

- Set a big goal in life, do not confuse goals with desires, a goal creates lifetime value in your life where desire doesn't.
- Don't waste your energy chasing your desires, invest your energy to chase a goal.
- Focus on one big goal at a time, never focus on your desires.
- Never expect too much from your one action; it can be disappointing. Try as many ways you can, to achieve your goal.
- Try everything to accomplish your goal, give your 100 percent.
- Take the necessary risks to accomplish your goal. Avoid unnecessary risk, go for easily available solutions.
- Motivation is important to achieve goals, and willpower is important to stay motivated to do work.

IX
Intention

Mahabharata is one of the most popular epics of Indian culture. This is the story of the cousins Pandavas and Kauravas. Kauravas were the 100 sons of Dhritarashtra and Pandavas were the 5 sons of King Pandu. Pandu abandoned the throne at an early age due to regret of killing a Rishi(sage) by mistake. Dhritarashtra became the king for the time until Pandu's son grew into an adult and became a king. Dhritarashtra's eldest son Duryodhana was an ambitious person, he wanted to become the king of Hastinapur, but the royal cabinet of the king was well aware of Duryodhana's bad intentions. So they chose Yudhishtra as a prince. It was decided that the eldest son of Pandu would be king. On the other hand, Duryodhana was not an easy giver of his dreams. He wanted to become the king at any cost, so he pressured his father, king Dhritrashtra to make him king. King Dhritrashtra agrees with Duryodhana. Dhritrashtra found the partition of the Kuru Rashtra as the only solution. Furthermore, King Dhritrashtra persuaded the royal cabinet to partition the kingdom of Hastinapur. Partition took place, and it was decided that the capital Hastinapur would be given to the Duryodhana. On the other hand, Pandavas would go to the Indraprastha (Delhi). Indraprastha was a deep forest having dangerous wild animals. Pandavas worked hard in the deep forest and established a great kingdom. They cleared the forest and cultivated the land. They worked hard to establish the great Kingdom of Indraprastha. Yudhishtra became the king of the Indraprastha. Yudhisthira became a very ethical king. The public was happy in his kingdom. His glory spread across the world. Everyone is living a happy life in Indraprastha. Shree Krishna advised them to perform Rajsuya Yagna. Pandavas accepted Shree Krishna's advice, and they organized the RajSuya yagna. This Yagna had many advantages, by performing this Yagna King Yudhisthira had to be declared as the Chakravarti Emperor (king of kings). It means there would be no one in the world to challenge emperor Yudhishthira after this Yagna. All kings and kingdoms had to obey Yudhishthira. Pandavas successfully performed RajSuya Yagna. On the other hand, Prince Duryodhana was not happy to see it. He was envied by his cousin brothers. He wanted to occupy the Indraprastha. So he chose an unethical way to occupy the Kingdom. He invited king Yudhishtra to the Hastinapur and arranged backgammon play. He challenged king Yudhshtra to play a backgammon game with him. Being a Chakravarti Emperor Yudhishtra couldn't refuse challenges, it would be against the dignity of a great king to refuse the challenge. So king Yudhisthira accepted the challenge. Bhishma (Grandfather of Kauravas and Pandavas) decided the rules of the game. Duryodhana requested Yudhishthira to allow Duryodhna's maternal uncle Shakuni to play on Duryodhna's behalf, Innocent King Yudhisthira Allowed him to do so. Shakuni was an expert gambler, and he was also a well-known cheater. He had many tricks to manipulate the game.

The game started and Shakuni started cheating in the game, he had developed two special kinds of dice. He could manipulate the game with those dice. The game started and as expected, king Yudhisthira started losing in-game. One by one, king Yudhistra started losing everything in gambling. Then unethical gambling started. Duryodhana and king Yudhishthira bet on their kingdoms. Yudhishthira bet on Indraprastha and Duryodhana bet on Hastinapur. Bhishma advised king Yudhishthira to stop, but he refused Bhishma's advice. Yudhishthira replied to Bhishma, that it would be against Chakravarti Emperor's dignity to escape from the challenge just because of fear of losing the throne of Indraprastha. As expected, King Yudhisthira lost the bet because of Shakuni's cheating techniques. Furthermore, Duryodhana approached king Yudhisthira to bet on his younger brothers, simultaneously whispering to Yudhisthira ``Remember the dignity of the great kuru dynasty, Kurus never escaped from any challenge". Yudhisthira agreed to bet on his brothers; he lost his brothers also in the bet. After that, he bet on himself in the play, and he lost. As per the deal, Yudhishtra accepted to become Duryodhna's slave. Duryodhana started showing his hate against them, and he ordered his younger brother Dhushasana to bring Yudhishthira's wife Draupadi to the Royal Assembly Court. Dushasana to drag Draupadi to the Royal Assembly Court. Envied, Duryodhana forced her to do sex with him in the Royal Assembly Court. Pandavas were powerful enough to kill them all, but they had become slaves, and they didn't want to disrespect their elder brother and his commitments, so they didn't stop Duryodhana. After seeing this humiliation of queen Draupadi, Bheema took the second Pandava oath to take revenge and kill all 100 sons of king Dhritrashtra. Other warriors, Bhishma, Dronacharya, Kripacharya, Vidur, and king Dhritrashtra remained silent because they all were in their dilemmas. They all fell into the trap of Duryodhana. They did not have clarity about their Dharma. So they believed that staying silent in front of their king is their DHARMA.

After a long humiliation, Queen Draupadi decided to curse Kauravas but suddenly Kauravas's mother, Queen Gandhari arrived at the Raj-Sabha (royal assembly court) and stopped Draupadi's humiliation. She requested Draupadi to not curse her sons. She offered her a compromise. Queen Gandhari ordered Duryodhana to return Pandavas' kingdom with respect, but Duryodhana was not ready to do that. He refused to return to Pandvas' kingdom. So his uncle Shakuni offered a deal to compromise. He offered a deal in a compromise that Pandavas have to go on the forest exile of 13 years. Shakuni Promised, that Duryodhana would return the kingdom to Pandavas, after this punishment. Duryodhana added one more condition, that Pandavas would live in the forest for 12 years and one year exile (agyatvas). Duryodhana's condition was that Pandavas' have to hide for last year, they should not be seen or identified by anyone. If they were seen or identified in that year, then they would have to repeat the cycle.

Pandavas spent 12 years in the forest, and after that, they successfully hid their identity for one year. Now it was Duryodhana's turn. He had to return their Kingdom to them as promised before. As Pandavas expected, Duryodhana refused to return to the kingdom of Indraprastha. Pandavas and other warriors tried to sort out this situation by talking to Duryodhana, but Duryodhana refused to return it to Pandavas. His warriors Bhishma, Daronacharya, Kripacharya, Karna all tried to convince him, but he didn't agree with them. Duryodhana challenged Pandavas to win the kingdom.

The main warriors of Duryodhana's army did not agree with him. They were compelled to obey Duryodhana's orders. Bhishma was compelled to support Duryodhana because he had taken the oath to serve for a lifetime to the kingdom of Hastinapur. Daronacharya was compelled by his son Ashwathama to support his friend Duryodhana. Kripacharya was compelled because he was the Rajguru(royal teacher) of the Kingdom, and he wanted to be loyal to his king. Karna was the eldest son of the Kunti and half-brother of the other five Pandavas, but he was also compelled to support Duryodhana because he was Duryodhana's best friend. These warriors were well-informed that Duryodhana was not a good person, so they didn't want to support Duryodhana, but they had to support him because of their commitments and loyalty.

These all warriors had the power to destroy the planets because they all were so powerful warriors. They all were undefeatable even Bhishma had the boon of **EUTHANASIA**, he could decide when to die, he had control over his death. He has the power to choose when to where to die. He was such an amazing warrior. Nobody had ever defeated him in his life. Duryodhana was also a great warrior.

On the other hand, Arjuna was the only archer from the Pandavas' side and Bheemsen (Bheema) was the only person with the power of ten thousand elephants. Bheemsen's favorite weapon was the mace, he was not an archer. Pandavas' other warriors were also strong, but not as strong as compared to the Kauravas warriors. They had only Arjuna to fight against legendary archers like Bheeshma, Dronacharya, Ashwathama, Kripacharya, Sharma, and Karna. On the other hand, they had only Bheema to fight against all 100 Kauravas brothers.

The strongest warrior Lord Krishna had decided to not fight in that war because lord Krishna wanted this war to be fair and an equal opportunity for both armies. He could kill both armies within a second. It would be a one-sided war if he had fought on either side.

Duryodhana knew all of these facts, that is why he was favoring war. He believed that his warriors were so strong, nobody could defeat his warriors except lord Krishna and lord Krishna had already decided to not fight. So he saw a win-win situation. He did not agree to negotiate with Pandavas, he had analyzed situations and had concluded that he would win the war.

After a long discussion and negotiations, Dhuryodhana's stubbornness won, and everyone agreed to war. They decided that war would take place in the divine land of Kurukshetra. It was decided that both Pandavas and Kauravas could call their allies for help. The entire world joined the war as per their opinions, some joined Pandavas and some joined Kauravas.

Everyone knew the power of Yadavas. Yadavas' king was Lord Krishna. Lord Krishna had an undefeated army named Narayani Sena(Lord Krishna's army). Both Pandavas and Kauravas wanted Lord Krishna to join their side. Both knew that Shree Krishna and his elder brother Lord Balaram were the most powerful warriors on the earth. Pandavas and Kauravas both knew the fact that Lord Krishna was the wisest man ever existed. Duryodhana and Arjuna both visited Dwarka (Lord Krishna's kingdom). Lord Krishna told them that "if he will fight from either side then the war will end in just a second and this will not be fair with both armies". That is why he had decided to not fight in the war. He said that his army can fight and Pandavas and Kuruvas can choose between him and his army. Lord Krishna said to Arjuna that he can advise them in war, but he will not fight against any army. He will not use any weapon in the war. So he gave him the freedom to choose. He could choose between his undefeated army or weaponless Lord Krishna. Duryodhana talks out between them and says "I came here first, so I must have the prerogative to choose first". Duryodhana asked for the Narayani army. But Shri Krishna refused to fulfill his wish first because he had seen Arjuna first, so he wanted to hear first from Arjuna. So he offered Arjuna to wish first. Arjuna chose Lord Krishna even without weapons because he knew Shri Krishna's wisdom. Arjuna chose wisdom over strength. Shri Krishna decided to become the charioteer of Arjuna to advise him in wartime.

Both sides formed large armies, where Pandavas had 7 akshauhini, and Kuruvas had 11 akshauhini on their side. (One akshauhini consisting of 21,870 chariots (Ratha); 21,870 elephants; 65,610 horses and 109,350 infantry as per the Mahabharata (Adi Parva 2.15-23).Thus, one akshauhini consisted of 218,700 warriors) These large armies were ready to fight a war.

As expected, Kauravas appointed Bhishma as their army commander. Where Pandavas appointed prince Drishtdyumana as their army commander. War began! Everyone was excited about the war. It was the war for justice for Queen Draupadi. As expected, Bhishma caused the death of many warriors of the Pandavas army. He was killing 10000 soldiers per day. He was the most powerful warrior of the Kauravas' side. He was aggressively killing Pandavas' armies. He damaged Pandavas' army a lot.

Only Lord Krishna was able to defeat Bhishma. Lord Krishna also knew how to defeat Bhishma. So he told the secret to Pandavas. Krishna told them that Bhishma is a proud warrior, and he does not attack women and trans genders. So Shikhandi(Queen Dropadi's trans-gendered sibling) can kill him because Shikhandi was a Trans gendered and Bhishma would not fight against Shikhandi. So they called Shikhandi into the battlefield, but Shikhandi couldn't kill Bhishma because his arrows did not have much force to pierce Bhishma's body. Dronacharya and other warriors were also trying to save unarmed Bhishma. Lord Krishna ordered Arjuna to save Shikhandi from those warriors. Arjuna came and started protecting Shikhandi. Then Lord Krishna ordered Arjuna to kill Bhishma also. Arjuna was not ready to kill unarmed Bhishma because Arjuna was also a proud warrior who did not attack unarmed warriors, and he also had an attachment with his grandfather Bhishma. Shree Krishna convinced him that he should perform his duty, and his only duty is to save his army and king. He should kill everyone who harms his army and king. Lord Krishna convinced him that it is not against pride to save the king and army. There was no reason to be attached to enemies' army commanders. He should not see Bhishma as his grandfather because he was on the battlefield and Bhishma was against him, so they should be treated only as anime, not as family members. On the 10th day, Arjuna and Shikhandi succeed in piercing Bhishma with arrows. As a result, Bhishma was no longer able to fight against Pandavas. He slept on the arrows.

Gradually, all warriors were killed by Pandavas. After 18 days of the war, Pandavas won the war and Yudhishtra became the King of Hastinapur.

Why Kurus Lost

The main reason for Pandavas' victory was their pure intention. Every soldier of the Pandavas army knew that they were on the side of Dharma. They knew that their purpose of fighting was divine. They were fighting with a pure heart. Their intention was very clear about the war that they have to win the war for the sake of justice. On the other hand, every warrior of the Kuru army was so strong, Dronacharya(Arjuna's Guru), Karna, Bhishma, Kripacharya, and Ashwathama, all were powerful archers. They all were as strong as Arjuna was. They all had powerful weapons like Brahmastra. (Oppenheimer, the father of the atomic bomb also mentioned

Bhramastra when he was asked about the first use of the Atomic bomb. Oppenheimer admitted that he had discovered an atom bomb for the first time in this age, in old ages it was already discovered and used, Oppenheimer mentioned a shloka of Geeta in his first interview after the first explosion).

Then why did they lose the war? Because all these warriors knew that they were supporting the wrong person. They knew that Duryodhana was a sinner and his ways were unethical. They were helping him because they all were bound in their commitments. Their intention to participate in the war was for the sake of their loyalty towards the kingdom. They have no intention to win the war. They all died in the battleground even though they fought with their full potential. The warriors of Kuru intended to prove their loyalty, not to win the war. They all prove their loyalty when they are martyred on the battlefield. Even though they were so strong but defeated by the Pandavas. The main reason is intention.

So what can we learn from this story? First; unethical ways of victory don't last long. Duryodhana won the kingdom of Indraprastha in gambling but lost it after 13 years in the war of justice. Second: We can learn that the intention matters a lot, if you and your partners don't have the same intention then the results are not going according to you. So one must have a pure intention of winning before starting work. If you are starting a business, your intention must be to be successful in the business. If one starts work just to try, then chances are high of failure. If someone starts with an intention like **either I will learn or either I will win, then definitely he will learn, he can never win.**

So a person should have clear intentions before starting a work that is what he wants to do. After a clear intention, work should be started with 100% energy and effort. A person should work hard for his goal.

Never Lose The Opportunity

Karna had the opportunity to kill Sahdeva, but he didn't kill him because he wanted to kill only Arjuna. He lost the opportunity. Arjuna was also losing the opportunity to kill Bhishma, but Lord Krishna told him to not lose the opportunity. Lord Krishna enlightened Arjuna with the divine knowledge of Bhagwat Geeta. If Arjuna had lost the opportunity to kill Bhishma, then war results could be different.

Arjuna was not ready to kill Karna, while Karna's charioteer wheel was in a pit. He said that it would be unethical to kill a weak enemy. Then Lord Krishna reminded him that Karna had also killed Abhimanyu (Arjuna's son) in an unethical way. Then Arjuna killed Karna.

Lord Krishna's message was clear ``one should never lose the opportunity``. One should never lose the opportunity to defeat his enemy. One should never lose the opportunity to go one step closer to his goals. Opportunities are rare in life and one should instantly grab the opportunity. If someone delays to grab the opportunity, then he may lose it.

Bill Gates

Once, a journalist asked Bill Gates about the secret of success? Bill Gates offered her a signed blank cheque. She got confused! She asked Bill Gates why he offered her a blank cheque. Bill Gates replied that this was the answer to your first question. Bill Gates said that she just lost the opportunity to become the richest woman in the world. Bill Gates said "I never missed an opportunity" like you just missed.

Keynotes

- Intention matters a lot to win a war, so be clear.
- Always do ethical work to achieve your goals, unethical ways may make you temporarily successful, but it doesn't last.

- Never lose an opportunity to achieve your goal.

X
Master Your Emotions

It is necessary to master emotions to be successful in life. Forget about the desires and become emotionally intelligent to accomplish goals. Goals need the right actions at the right time. You may lose many opportunities because of emotions. So you need to learn to be stable in every situation. Stable in grief and happiness. A stable person can make stable decisions that can lead to success. If a person makes good decisions in a good mood, then his chances are high to make bad decisions in a bad mood. So it is important to always stay stable.

Over Enthusiasm

India has a glorious history. Lord Rama's father King Dashrath was a valor king. He is remembered as a great warrior. In the battle of Suras-Asuras(Dev-Danav), King Dashrath took Indra's (king of Devas/Asuras) side, King Dashrath got severe injuries in the war, Queen Kekkei showed her valor and saved king Dashratha. In the end, Indra and Dashratha won the battle. King Dashratha was impressed by his queen Kekkei. He was feeling proud to have such a queen. He was extremely happy to have such a valor queen. In enthusiasm; He promised two Verdana(boon) to Queen Kekkei. Queen Kekkei said that she will use these boons when she needs them. She reserved her prerogative of two boons from the king. After many years, the king had four sons Rama, Laxman, Bharatha, and Shatrughna. They all were great warriors and wise. Lord Rama was the eldest, wisest and valorous one, King Dashrath wanted to make him king.

One day, King Dasharatha feels that he has grown old. He thinks that he has reached a ripe age. His only wish was to see Rama as a King. Rama was not only the eldest but also the most capable prince.

Dasharatha took counsel with his adviser, ministers, and elders. It was decided that Rama will be their new king. All approved and acclaimed the proposal, cheered in one voice," Make Rama the king the very next morning."

Thus, unanimously, Rama was declared king of Ayodhya.

Immediately, guru Vishwamitra and other elders were given directions to prepare for the coronation ceremony. Dasharatha sent for Rama and told him that he would be crowned the next morning. The news cheered all in the palace. Rama went to his mother and hoped for news. Kaushalya was meditating and Sita and Laxman waited on her. Lord Rama and Sita fasted, kept the night vigil, and spent all their time in prayer and meditations.

Kaikeyi too was glad to know about Rama's Coronation. She loved Rama as her son Bharata. She had a hunch-backed maidservant named Manthara. She came to Kaikeyi and poisoned her mind, arousing deep feelings of jealousy against Rama and Kausalya. Mantra said," O unfortunate and thoughtless queen, Rama will be king tomorrow, and you are a waiting-maid with folded hands on Kaushalya as I am yours. And your beloved son Bharata will become Rama's errand boy."

Swept off her feet by Manthara's evil counsel, Kaikeyi said," O maid, you are the best of my well-wishers, Now I can see through the king, my husband's evil designs and plans to dethrone me from my position of privilege."

Gradually, Kaikeyi's doubts grew strong and then stronger. Completely misled by the Manthara, she forgot her love for Rama, she made up her mind to ask for two boons the king had granted her long ago.

Blissfully unaware of this sudden turn of events, king Dasharatha came to Kaikeyi's palace to give the happy news of Rama's crowning to his most favorite queen. His queen remembered him, her two boons. King said, "Tell me what is your wish, and it will be fulfilled instantly, swear by my dharma your pleasure will be done."

She asked the king to give his word and to swear by Rama. Intent on evil, the lady then said," Grant me my two boons you promised long ago, Consecrate and make my son Bharatha king of Ayodhya in place of Rama. And for the second boon, send Rama to the forest in exile for fourteen years".

These cruel words stunned Dasharatha. Then he became senseless. Regaining his consciousness, he heaved a deep sigh and again went into a swoon struck with grief, With great efforts, he again came to his senses and pleaded with Kaikeyi with folded hands to spare Rama and his life, for Rama's departure to the forest would kill him. But the queen remained firm and unmoved. The king's sobs, tears, begging, and prayers on the knees rather hardened her cruel heart more and more. Dasharatha repeated weeping, "Let's Bharata have the crown and kingdom, but don't exile Rama, the best among men, my only refuge. I shall die the moment I don't see him. Grant me only this prayer".

Kaikeyi remained silent to the king's supplications. The king, remembering the dreadful oath he had taken in the name of Rama and Kaikeyi's firm resolve to send Rama into exile, fell again on the ground and lapsed into a swoon. Kaikeyi sent Rama. Rama came and saw his father struck with grief and his face parched. The king could not utter a word because his throat was choked with sobs and grief. Rama stood stunned at this miserable sight of his father and said, "Tell me mother, please, why is my father so dejected? Have I displeased him? Has anybody else done something or said something improper? Asked in great anxiety, why is he in such a gloomy state, I never saw him before?"

Kaikeyi said, "The king is neither ill nor has anybody displeased him. But he dare not speak something, which is unpleasant to you, whom he holds most dear. You should carry out what he has promised me. He granted me two boons but now demurs to fulfill them. If you swear to fulfill these, I may tell you what they are."

"Tell me, mother, what has my father promised you? I will do that, I promise. You know, I never tell lies," said Rama.

Having got the desired assurance, the queen said, "The king has promised to concrete Bharata as a King and to send you away into exile for fourteen years. Now keep your promise to enable your father to honor his word and depart to the forest this very day."

These words did not pain the noble Rama at all. In a firm voice, he replied, "I will redeem my father's pledge and your boons will be fulfilled. I leave for the Dandaka forest.

Greatly delighted at these noble words of Rama, Kaikeyi was abundantly reassured. However, she urged Rama's early departure. The king had heard all that had passed there, but being unable to speak anything, he cried faintly, "Oh Rama! Oh, miserable me."

Rama raised his father and then took his leave respectfully. Rama, the heroic soul, went straight to his mother followed by Lakshman. There was no trace of sadness or anger; he wore a sweet smile as usual. Such was his fortitude and devotion to duty and Dharma. He departed to Dandaka forest with his wife and brother Laxmana.

In Ayodhya, King Dashratha having succumbed to this pressure, Dasharatha, plagued by regrets, took to his sickbed, where he eventually died of grief.

Why Is Lord Rama Hero Of Billions Of Hearts?

Here we can learn from both Lord Rama and King Dasaratha, In over enthusiasm the king promised two boons to his queen Kekkei that cost his life to end. On the other hand, Lord Rama was calm and stable in every situation. He successfully spent 14 years in the forest and won a battle against King Ravana in Lanka. Rama stayed calm and remained stable in every situation; he never regretted any action. He never failed in anything in his life. Lord Rama lived a legendary life, and he is the hero of billions of hearts. He always remained stable in every situation. He never took any bad decision out of over-enthusiasm, nor took a bad decision because of grief.

We must learn to better control our emotions to accomplish big goals. Because big goals need the right decisions at the right time. **An unstable person can never make the right decisions at the right time**. We must have better control over emotions, so we never make bad decisions, and we never regret that. So our decisions never fill our hearts with grief. It is important to understand that **a person who can't control his emotions in happiness won't be able to control his grief.**

Enthusiasm gives us the energy to do everything. Enthusiasm is really important for our life, but at the same time over-enthusiasm leads to wrong decisions. An achiever always has a stable mind. An achiever always stays calm and stable. To be an achiever, you must learn to be stable in joy and grief, winter and summer. Stabilizing yourself is the best way to be happy in your life, decisions you take in enthusiasm can drag you into trouble.

Queen Kekkei misused the king's boons that were promised to her in enthusiasm. **Most of the bad decisions are taken in an extremely good or bad mood.** So that is why one should always be stable in every situation. So it can give a stable life.

Stabilize Emotions

You may have heard that **"you should not take any decision while you are extremely happy or extremely sad". But the golden rule is "you should not be extremely happy and extremely sad".** You should always control your emotions. Because if you feel emotions extremely, it leads to feeling every emotion at an extreme level. Because your brain makes changes within. The brain develops the habit of feeling everything extremely when you feel extreme emotions. The habit of feeling emotions deep is useless because it has only losses to give you. That's why: You should always be in a stable situation in your life. So you can be successful in every aspect of your life.

You may have heard many people complain that they are not comfortable in many aspects of their life. They always complain about the situations, about people and society. The main reason for their unhappiness is their unstable emotions. They instantly feel happiness as they meet their friends and loved ones. They feel sad when they are alone. This all happens because they are emotionally weak and unstable people.

What is the need to grow these emotions in your life? These emotions can't give you anything in your life. These emotions only have drawbacks for you. These emotions only stop you from being successful and limitless. As we discussed before, if a person feels extreme happiness, then definitely he feels sadness at its peak. If an over-enthusiastic athlete works so hard to win a gold medal, he fails to win a gold medal. Then chances are high that he might never practice again, never work to win a gold medal. If an exceptional person starts to work again to win a gold medal then he would be less dedicated towards his goal because he will feel disappointed inside to do anything, he will lack energy and motivation.

Stabilizing emotion doesn't mean not feeling happy in life, rather it means always being happy in every situation. A person who has stable emotions doesn't need anything extraordinary to make him happy. Happiness comes from inside him. He doesn't need anything to excite him, he never feels bored. He doesn't need people to entertain him, he enjoys himself. He doesn't need motivation from the outside; his goal is enough to motivate him. A person who has stable emotions never goes into depression because he never feels extreme sadness. His decisions never drag him in regret and grief because he always makes stable decisions. By stabilizing emotions a person enjoys countless benefits it is not possible to write all benefits here, but if I describe the benefits of stabilizing emotions in a single line then it will be **"ultimate happiness and accomplishments of every goal in life"**.

To stabilize emotions, a person should practice meditation, Pranayam. Pranayam is a very powerful practice, Pranayam is not just breathing practice, it is more than that, it also helps in stabilizing emotions. A person should control his anger and sadness by not thinking about the cause. These simple techniques will grow a person's level, and he can successfully control his emotions.

The human heart is agile by nature, one should not let it do whatever it wants to do, one should try to stabilize it, by force or whatever it takes. **If you win your Heart, it becomes your best friend and if you lose to it, then it becomes your worst enemy.** To stabilize emotions, controlling your heart is important. To control your heart, just do a single practice. Whenever it says anything to you, don't do that. Stop your heart's arbitrary. Stop listening to every unnecessary demand of the heart. Try to control it every time. **A person who wins his heart is the king of his heart and a person who follows his heart blindly and does everything that heart says, he is the slave of his heart.** So be a king of your heart and control it, do not be a slave of your heart, don't let it control you.

Self Control

A company had a business deal with another company of 10 crores. An employee who had data was 1 hour late due to traffic. So his manager screamed at him as he arrived. He abused him and didn't let the employee speak. The employee got sad, and he typed his resignation letter and resigned. After seeing the resignation, the manager realized that he had made a huge mistake and tried to stop the employee. But the employee was extremely sad. He immediately left the office. No one had abilities to substitute him, no one was able to do his work. The company lost the deal without that employee. Because of the manager's anger, the company lost the deal. Business partners blacklisted the company because the company didn't deliver what it promised. The company lost its image in the market. The company faced huge losses because of this single incident. Lack of self-control costs them a lot. It took 10 years to come back on track for that company.

If the manager had controlled himself, then the company could get the deal even after a delay. He could cut that employee's salary if he wanted to punish him. The company bore huge losses because of the manager's anger. A wise man can understand that it is very important to control anger.

Self-control is essential. A person can avoid huge losses by controlling himself.

Always take a deep breath and think about the situation, what could be the consequences of the explosion of anger. Just analyze the situation for a few minutes. If you are feeling like screaming at your wife, then you should think that this can end your relationship. If you are feeling like screaming at your best friend, then you should think that this moment can ruin a friendship. Every time you think about the consequences, you save yourself from huge losses. Try this to control your anger, and you have already won in many aspects of life. Defeat the anger and control your life.

You should always think with a calm mind. Your every decision and every step should be calculated. Don't regret later, control anger first.

Gautam Adani's Self Control

Gautam Adani is the CEO and MD of the Adani group. Once, his employee made a mistake worth millions of dollars. Everyone was expecting that he would be fired. Adani summoned him to his office and after a few minutes, Adani announced that the employee will not be fired. Adani said in his declaration, that this employee has made a loss in Adani's company, and he has learned from his mistake by using Adani's resources now Adani will not let competitors take the benefit of his employee's experience. Further, Adani said: Mistakes are expensive. Rivals should not take advantage of your mistake, but it doesn't mean you have to keep a loser employee forever with you, if the employee can't take lessons from the mistake then he must be replaced.

There is no reason to abuse anyone. If someone doesn't agree with you because he has his identity and opinion, you also may disagree with him, but there's no reason for saying wrong words about him.

Always remember, anger comes in a favorable situation. Because people only get angry according to their comfort, for example, if a senior inspector beats a criminal, the criminal does not get angry and doesn't beat the inspector back because he knows that the inspector can harm him in a lot of ways by law. Many times people underestimate the situation and show their anger to their subordinates. But later they fall into a worse situation. So never underestimate situations. Never misbehave with anyone, and never show anger to anyone. Respect people and talk properly with gratitude with everyone that everyone deserves.

There is no reason to get angry at anyone. You should always be calm and save energy to do something productive. Your good behavior can save you from losses, it can create more opportunities for you.

Shree Krishna says **"Unnecessary desires, Anger and Greed are the doors of hell"**. These are the worst enemies of mankind.

Understand people

People are the biggest assets, so always try to understand your biggest assets. We are social beings, and we need to communicate everywhere with people. First understand people to be understood. I believe that it is impossible to be successful without having good relations with people.

An achiever never imposes his decisions on other people. He always convinces people. An achiever never tries to shut a person up, by speaking loudly. An achiever never tries to suppress anyone.

Reaction

In February 1998, when Bill Gates was in Brussels, Belgium, to visit European Union officials, he was struck in the face by two people with a cream pastry--a cake back to back, while he was entering a government building to give a speech on education.

Guess what was the reaction of Bill Gates; Bill didn't even say a single word. He just went to the washroom, washed his face, and attended his scheduled meeting without any negative expressions on his face. He calmly entered the meeting room and finished his meeting successfully. Everyone knows Bill Gates, and it's easy to imagine what he could do with the cake thrower. But Bill Gates even didn't file a lawsuit against him. He said nothing about that incident, he did nothing to take revenge.

This is a perfect example of a proactive person who didn't react to anything unnecessary. Bill Gates didn't let the other people spoil his mood. While I was watching the video I was thinking at the time if someone would throw a cake on my face, I would have beaten him as a spontaneous reaction.

Bill Gates has awesome control over his reaction. He is not a slave of his reaction, his reactions are his slave. He didn't know that he would be smashed, but he didn't panic in the situation, he was stable, and he created a great image. Bill Gates made thousands of fans after this reaction and self-control.

If a common man were at Bill Gates' Place, then he would have beaten the cake thrower and ruined his public image.

If you throw a cake on a person's face, whose net worth is only $100, then he will say these kinds of words "hey you don't know me", "you don't know my father", "you will pay for it", "you don't know my status".

We can learn from Bill Gates; be in your control in every situation. Always be ready for unfavorable circumstances. Like, Bill Gates didn't know that someone was going to throw a cake on his face, so he wasn't able to control the other person's actions, but he was able to control his reaction.

Successful people don't waste their time thinking about negative people. Successful people only focus on their own goals. They don't waste their energy on useless people. They don't react to stupid people.

Keynotes

- Never be extremely happy nor extremely sad.
- Always be stable in life, stabilize your emotions.
- Take a deep breath in anger and think about the losses of your anger, then talk wisely.
- Situations can be unexpected and worse at any time, always be ready to deal with unexpected circumstances.
- Never take everything personally, don't waste focus on useless battles or ego.
- If you win your Heart, it becomes your best friend and if you lose to it, then it becomes your worst enemy.

XI
Desires

Desires

A Family with expensive mobiles- A family that migrated to India, They live in a two-room set on rent. They are six brothers, and they are such hardworking people. Some of them work for a daily wage and some of them are bulldozer operators. Their combined income is almost 2000 dollars per month. They could buy a house, they earn enough to buy a house, but they buy expensive mobile phones and other gadgets. They think that expensive mobile phones will make them happy, or maybe they will look rich after buying expensive mobile phones. They want to be with the trend. So they purchase every new and trendy mobile phone. They buy every new gadget available in the market, new TV, new refrigerators, etc. I asked one of them, "What is the use of this expensive mobile in your life? How is it important to you? I have seen you buying every new gadget. He simply replied that it's trendy and cool, it has the latest features in it. I asked, "Do you use those features? He replied: sometimes! I said ok!. Then I asked him about his savings, he replied, "I am not rich", "I don't have that much money". "I can't save". "We have a big family to feed". That's why we are not able to save a penny. He told me more reasons behind his situation.

I was thinking that he'll have money to buy a new mobile phone. **People who can never control their desires can never accomplish anything big in their life.**

Unnecessary Desires can become habits

I remember in my college days, I was a fit and healthy boy. I had a desire to eat tasty fast food and junk food. I became habitual of unhealthy food. I used to eat pizza, burgers, hot dogs, and junk foods daily. After some years I started facing some serious issues of obesity, and other digestion-related issues. My friend started to call me obese, chubby, motu, etc. But I was helpless because I was not able to control my desire to eat. Every night I thought that it was my last day, I would quit from the very next day. But days were passing, and I was saying the same lines daily. " It was last night man, you have strong willpower you will not eat from tomorrow. Then I realized that I should start controlling myself and take small steps. So first I stopped eating snacks and junk food. It was hard for me. I used to eat junk food, but somehow I controlled myself, and the next day I stopped eating pizza and other fast foods. I lost 10 kg weight within three months just by controlling myself. Yes, it is that easy, If you do it with commitment.

We humans have endless desires, if we buy a jet, then we'll have a desire to buy a luxurious one. If we buy a mobile phone, then we'll have a desire to buy an expensive mobile. If someone eats pizza then he'll have the desire to eat more pizza, (if someone thinks that he will satisfy his desires of eating pizza then he is putting petrol on fire). You must understand the difference between capacity and desire. Because if one eats pizza today and says" He doesn't have the desire to eat more pizza. This is because he can't eat more. This is the only limit of his capacity for that day, his desire is still unsatisfied. The next day, he will eat again. The same happens with sex. One can finish his energy and capacity for the day but can never satisfy desires for sex by doing more and more sex. It is impossible to put out the fire with the help of gasoline. If you want to put out the fire, then you should attack the source of the fire.

Rapists are those people who do not control their unnecessary desires of sex. They do everything to fulfill their desires. They do not try to control their sexual desires, which is why they commit crimes. Similarly, a person who always stays high in intoxication is also a slave of their desires. These people can never achieve success in their life because they do not have any control over their unnecessary desires.

Story of a king

A king tried to satisfy his sexual desire, he married 390 women. Besides this he had many sex slaves, he had a choice of doing sex with different countries sex slaves. He used to swim with thousands of nude women. He had created an environment where he can do sex every time with the woman of his choice. He wanted to satisfy his sexual desires.

He used to take many herbs and medicines to increase his sexual capacity. He had many sexual consultants in his palace. He liked to do sex in different ways. He had many Vaidyas, Doctors, and Hakeem to give him medicines and herbs to increase his sexual capacity and stamina. Everything was going fine, but at the age of 40, he started facing issues related to his sexual capacity. Doctors, vaidyas, and Hakeem tried to revive his sexual capacity with medicines, and it worked for some time. But at last, every doctor and Hakeem's technique stopped working on him. He lost his stamina and power, both. His body was not able to support his sexual desires. He still had the desire of doing a lot of sex, but his body was not able to do that.

He died at the age of 48 years because of depression. The cause of his depression was his unfulfilled desires. He got depressed because of his unfulfilled desires. **This is what happens with every person who runs after his desires**. King dedicated his entire life to sex, but in the end, he died because he was not able to do sex. A man who only did sex in his entire life, even he was not able to satisfy his desire for sex, so how can we expect to satisfy our desires? Now, a wise man can understand the trap of unnecessary desires.

If a person does sex to satisfy his sexual desire, then he will have more desire for sex. If one thinks his desire will be satisfied after buying a thing, then he must understand that he will have more desires of buying new things. This process continues as man tries to satisfy desires. If one desire gets fulfilled then your desire will be back in a bigger picture, it will force you to fulfill the next big desire.

Use it to benefit you

So why not fulfill desires that will add value in life. Why not use this energy to achieve something great. You can work to fulfill desires that can add value in life. A burning desire for success. A burning desire to accomplish your goal. A desire for knowledge, A desire for fitness, A desire that leads you closer to your goal. You should only focus on desires whose results will matter at the end, whose results can create an impact in your life. Your desire should match up with your goal.

How To Control Unnecessary Desires?

The Worst way of getting rid of unnecessary desires is trying to satisfy them. **"Desires are similar to a fire, people want to put out the fire with the help of petrol"**. Nobody can put out the fire with gasoline. Gasoline can kindle a fire.

If you have an unnecessary desire then think about your goal, now think about your desire where it stands, will it help you to become what you want to be. Think about the legends who have achieved great goals in life, will you desire to help you to become a legend too? To control your desires, never satisfy them. You should control every small unnecessary desire to achieve awesome control (like, do not eat junk food if you have a strong desire to eat, do not watch porn, stop watching erotica) Don't buy unnecessary accessories from the market. Try to control each unnecessary desire. After some time, you'll realize that you have achieved awesome self-control. One should hustle for goals to control unnecessary desires. Without a goal, a person runs after useless desires. Unnecessary Desires will never let you succeed. Unnecessary desires are the enemy of success. **Unnecessary desires are the worst enemies of the goals.** Unnecessary desires distract a person's focus from goal to desire. **A person who chases his unnecessary desires can never have time to achieve his goals.** A person who chases his unnecessary desires can never accomplish his goals in life.

Benefits of controlling desires

The king would have lived a long life if he didn't have the desire of doing a lot of sex. Even he would be able to enjoy more sex in his long life.

If those migrants had control over their desires, they could have their own house. But they just have to follow the trend, and they just have to buy trendy accessories. Many people do the same thing. They spend money on unnecessary desires and regret later for it. They don't learn anything from their mistakes, and they jump in the race of satisfying their new unnecessary desire. Desires come in endless sequences. And the type of desire matters, what you fulfill. If you fulfill an unnecessary desire, then it brings more unnecessary desires. If you fulfill your desire for success, then more desires of achieving success come to you. If you fulfill a desire to accomplish a small goal, the desire of accomplishing bigger goals comes to you. Always choose wisely and never let unnecessary desires win over you. Desires are important to succeed in life, but unnecessary desires never let the person succeed.

You can save money by controlling desires, you can become healthy and fit. You can have long-lasting love if you control desire. The most essential thing is that you can be successful in your life and accomplish goals in life if you control your desires.

Nobody is going to ask you in your 60s which mobile phone you had at the age of 25" Nobody is going to ask you about your swag. A swag of 25 will not matter for your children, only your wealth will matter. Their school or college will not ask about your 20s girlfriends and cool friends. Things that matter: how much bank balance you have, How successful you are, your personality, and how much knowledge you have.

If you successfully control your desires, then you become unstoppable in your life. You can accomplish every goal in your life.

How can you save money if you don't have control over your desires? Your unnecessary desires will never let you become rich and successful. Because a person who is driven by his unnecessary desires only wants enjoyment. He only wants to have fun. As he'll have some money and his unnecessary desire will say buy this thing man you deserve it, it'll represent your status. If you'll save some money after your monthly expenses then your desires will say yeah man, go for a trip you should explore the world. If he'll have a bonus, his unnecessary desire will say yes man this is the right time you should buy a new cell phone, your mobile is outdated.

You and your goal will lose every time, and your desires will win if you don't control unnecessary desires. Desires say, savings? Ah! Boring. Investment? Ah! You have a lot of time to do that, so let me enjoy this time.

Your unnecessary desires have a pit for all of your money and resources. You can never be rich if you can not control them, **"money is power and if you are wasting it everywhere, you will become a weak person" money is power, if you save it, it gives you more power. "If you save money, money will save you"**.

Nature has the power of balancing everything. **If you save money, then nature will make money to save you because it has to create balance. If you waste your resources, then it will also waste you.**

Keynotes

- Unnecessary desires are obstacles in the way of achieving a goal.
- Desires can never be satisfied by fulfilling them, it always comes back in a more destructive picture.
- Desire is like a fire, and some want to put out the fire with the help of petrol.
- A person can achieve everything in his life if he controls his desires.

Part Three

USE ENERGY AND SUBCONSCIOUS MIND TO ACHIEVE
EVERYTHING IN LIFE

XII
Mind and Its Powers

Powerful Brain

Brain's qualities are much superior to the imagination. The mind can also control the physical world's circumstances as it controls our body. To understand the concept of powers of the subconscious mind, first, we need to understand the power of the entire human brain. When I talk about the brain it means the entire brain, not only the subconscious mind or conscious mind because one is useless without another. Your entire brain is powerful. But some people have represented the conscious mind as a villain. They have shown it as the biggest obstacle between you and your goals. This kind of shit is spread on the internet. They have made a conscious mind culprit, they show the programming of the subconscious mind as a disaster.

But you need to understand that these are equally important to make you successful in your life. One's task is thinking and creating new ideas, another's task is making them real.

Your subconscious mind controls your body, it controls your nervous system, blood flow, eye blinking breathing process, and it also controls your balance when you walk.

On the other hand, your conscious mind helps you in understanding things, learning new skills, talking wisely, influencing people, thinking about new ideas, and differentiating between reality and dreams.

Your conscious mind helps you to learn how to drive a car, once you learn it, then your subconscious mind saves the data to automate the process, and you become an expert in it. The subconscious mind saves the data provided by the conscious mind. It saves every step and learning in detail. It saves data on how to change gear and braking. It saves data for thousands of kilometers to make you an expert. During learning, you need to keep in mind to gear up and gear down for some days. Whenever you see a deep curve, your conscious mind alerts you to down the gear. It happens to you until your subconscious mind fully trains itself and saves every piece of information to automate the driving process. Once the subconscious mind learns everything, then it automates itself to drive. After automation, you don't have to worry about gear up and gear down or brake, it just happens automatically. Your conscious mind helps to program your subconscious mind to automate things. Once the subconscious mind has all the required data, it becomes easy and obvious to work easily without thinking about it. This awesome combination of minds makes a person successfully learn something and automate that. This awesome combination of both minds can help us a lot to accomplish goals. Both are needed to work properly in combination.

Amazing Abilities of Mind

I would like to explain the existence of ghosts because there couldn't be a better way to explain the abilities of the human mind. Every living being has a mind, but the human mind is special, it has special powers and abilities. Humans can imagine things at that level, no other beings can. Humans can do invention, no other living being can do this. Humans are the wisest beings on this planet.

Only humans can see ghosts. Not a single animal other than a human can see ghosts. We humans have a fear of ghosts and the reason is our mind. Only we humans can see the ghosts and that is why we have fear of ghosts. A person who has a fear of ghosts or is curious about ghosts must read it carefully. I guarantee you will understand the ghosts.

Do Ghosts Exist?

Human death is the universal truth. People believe that death is obvious. Humans do not have much fear of natural death because we all know that it is the reality of humans. "One day we all have to die naturally. That is why humans do not have negative, powerful, and sad emotions related to natural death. No one thinks that natural death is unlucky. Nobody wants to die before natural death. Humans are neutral for natural death. Everyone wants to live 100% life.

On the other hand, every human has fear of unexpected and unnatural death. That is why we have negative emotions and negative energy for unnatural death. Whenever a person dies an unnatural death because of accident, suicide, murder, and disease. He feels the worst emotions at the time of death. These are the most painful deaths. These people become the worst memory for the universe. These people feel extreme sadness at the time of death. They have extremely negative energy at the time of death.

So when a scared person goes through the place where he had heard ghost stories. He remembers that story. By remembering the horror story related to that place, his awareness goes in that direction. His energy flows in that direction. He starts concentrating on the horror history of that place. His mind starts focusing on that person who had died there. Because of fear, a scared person's concentration level increases. He starts thinking about the person who died at that place. This increased concentration increases focus. The focus becomes laser-sharp. The person only thinks about that person who had died there. His fear does not let him distract from the situation, and his focus gets deeper and deeper on the situation. Finally, an innocent and unaware person who does not know the power of focus and consciousness accesses the memory of the universe about that place. His mind starts to play the memory of the universe like a movie, and his mind starts hallucinating. He sees the death of that person in the universe's memory. He accesses the universe's memory related to that place. His mind senses and feels that negative energy. Universe has a bad and negative memory and energy about that place, which was emitted in grief by a sad person. This energy and memory scare a focused person. Because it is an unusual and extremely sad emotion and the energy related to that emotion is extremely negative, that is why it feels so bad after sensing that energy. You may have noticed that people who believe in ghosts only see and feel ghosts in many haunted places. People who do not believe in ghosts, never see ghosts, not even in haunted places. Have you ever thought, why does it happen? This happens because, a person who believes in ghosts, his consciousness, and focus is more likely to explore the haunted incident. His mind naturally starts to focus on the ghost. As a result, they access the bad memories of the universe, related to that place.

This is how a person sees ghosts. The emotion and energy were extremely strong behind the haunted place when it was emitted. That is why it is easily sensible for a focused person. This energy can be easily caught by a focused person.

Ghosts Do Not Exist

In real life, there are no ghosts. Neither existed ever before. It is only the power of the human mind that can help to reach everywhere with focus. Everything that exists in the universe is also possible to see with focus.

A drunk person rarely sees ghosts. Because a drunk person can not have a focused mind, that is why he can't focus on the ghosts. Intoxicants don't let him access the memory of the universe. A drunk person can't stabilize his mind. He has multiple thoughts. He has many distracting thoughts, he can't concentrate and focus. This happens with every drunk person. That is why drunk people are less likely to see a ghost.

Your Mind Is The key

Your mind is the key to access to the universe's memory. It is the same process as a mobile phone accessing the memory card's files. This is the ability of your mind. You may think that mobile phone and memory card comparison is not appropriate for the brain because they have electricity, software and for memory, there are metals and chemicals. The answer is: the **brain also has an awesome software that we call the mind**, the brain also contains metals, chemicals, and energy within.

When the first time the audiotape was invented, it was **a thin steel wire. Gradually,** it shifted to a plastic backing coated with a thin layer of tiny particles of magnetic powder. As you can see, the first choice for the audio equipment was steel, not plastic because at that time we did not have a technology that could read data from plastic backing coated storage. Similarly, when a memory chip and memory reader was developed. It was developed with the best materials, like with the best suitable metal, with the best suitable chemicals. After some years to make it cost-effective researchers tried to make it with cheaper options. And now we can see a memory card that is made of cheaper material and stores data better than older memory chips. A plastic reel in a cassette can store data. The cassettes are made up by using non-metal. It is enough to clear that metals are not important to store data. Science has developed only to this level that we can store data in cassettes, DVDs, and chips.

The universe is more advanced than human-made equipment. It stores data everywhere, even in the environment, in stones, and metals. The human mind is a thousand times ahead and more powerful than these devices like mobile phones, laptops, and DVD players. The human mind can access the universe's data by focusing on that. This is the power of the focused mind.

As metals store data, similarly the universe stores data. Each part of the universe saves data, environment, trees, stones, and spoils everything. Everything has a memory, only we don't know how to access that. We don't have physical equipment to open and see the data that is stored in this universe. That is why we think that this universe does not store any data within. But almighty God has created everything perfect. He has given us a mind that can access all the universal data.

The human mind can access the memory of the universe. The Human mind can see everything that happened in the past in this universe. We can catch the thoughts. We can catch the memories that are recorded in this universe. The human brain is the equipment to play the memory of the universe.

We, humans, are fickle-minded. We don't want to focus sharply. That is why it seems difficult for us to access the universe's data. That is why we look for easy solutions to access the data. We discovered every easy way to transfer data to our next generation. In great Vedic civilization, great Vedic knowledge was passed from Guru to Disciple through verbal teaching and the disciple had to learn it, so he could use it and pass it to his disciples, in this process the brain had to store the data, so it could be called a soft copy of the data. So humans found it difficult to store large amounts of data in the mind. So humans discovered writing methods to make it easy. Then humans started various ways to note it down. Humans invented scripts that could be learned easily. Humans set different shapes in scripts to define different words and things. Then humans started using copper plates to write, which we call copper plate inscriptions, and later to make it easy and convenient humans invented papers to transfer store data easily. Humans found simple and easy ways to store and decode data. And people who could decode that could easily understand what is written on that paper. So here humans shifted soft copy to hard copy of the data.

This is how humans started to make it easy to store and decode data easily. As technology grew up, humans felt that it is difficult to write and read all data, so we discovered more easy ways to store and decode data. Then we discovered the audio, video, and other formats to store data and to access it, we invented devices accordingly. Humans discovered devices to create, store and decode soft electronic copies of data. This time, humans moved to soft copies from the hard copies of data.

Humans created everything according to comfort. So now it is clear that storing the data and accessing that data is not only related to a single device or mechanism, but it is related to human brain abilities. So it is important to understand that we humans can access any type of data, it is just we need a mechanism or equipment to access that data.

Trikaldarshi

We have a mechanism to access the universal data that is our mind. Universe has its storage where it saves everything. Great ancient sages and Maharishis had an ultra-focused mind, so they could access this universal memory, that is why they were called **TRIKALDARSHI** (a person who knows everything). Great sages could give answers to every question, they had answers to every question. They could enter into the father's house, the universal consciousness. This universal consciousness has answers to every question. So great ancient sages knew everything that the universe has. Every human has the same ability to access universal consciousness and its data. It only takes a focused mind and knowledge. In universal consciousness, you can find everyone's thoughts and memories. There are many great thinkers, sages, prophets, and successful people's thoughts and memories, so you can find answers to every question there. You can have unlimited access to unlimited knowledge. You don't need to spend thousands of dollars on that. You can access it for free, with a focused mind you can access infinite knowledge and everything that the universe has. This universe has memory and your mind can access it. Your mind can enter into the universal consciousness. This is the power of the human mind. The mind can access anywhere, and it has the power to create everything.

Father's House

According to ancient Vedas, universal consciousness is the father's house, and we can enter the father's house by focusing on that. We all humans believe in God, some people call themselves atheists, but they also believe in God. **A person who believes in himself is also a believer because he believes in him and he is also part of this universe and the universe is the part of God.** According to the great ancient Vedas, God is everywhere, in every person, and everything, so if a person believes in himself or any other person, he believes in God. I am not against atheist people, but they are also part of this universal consciousness. Their consciousness is also connected with universal consciousness. This is the house of the father. If a person focuses on entering into the father's house, he enters into the father's house. He can see everything in his father's house. The human mind is the key to entering the father's house. Once you enter the father's house, you can see infinite wisdom and great thoughts there. You can see every memory of this universe. Everything will be visible to you if you enter the father's house.

I know you are not interested to see everything in the father's house. It also takes a lot of focus to do so, but you can find answers to every question in your father's house. Father has the answer to every question. You don't have to do something extraordinary to enter into the father's house. You just have to focus on the answers. Your mind will open the doors of answers for you. Your mind will obey your orders and only explore your answers in the father's house. So focus on the solutions to your problem with your full energy, your focus should be laser-sharp, so your mind will open the doors for you. Your mind is the key to infinite wisdom and possibilities, use it to grow in your life, use it to achieve your goals.

Divine Places And Their Energy

Whenever a person focuses on god, he naturally focuses on the positive and divine energy, and he gets little access to the universal memory related to that place. And the level of divine energy a person feels depends on his devotion. Because being more devoted makes people more focused. By focusing on God, people naturally focus on good memories of the universe related to that place. Because of deep focus, their mind accesses the good memories of that place and people feel blessed. The more he focuses on God, the more he has access to universal memory related to the good things and God's energy and feeling good. The more a person feels divine energy, the more he absorbs that. That is why religious scriptures have mentioned indirectly that **"never go to the divine place with an atheist"**. They knew the concept of a focused mind and energy. They knew that a single percent of negative energy can distract a devotee's focus. This is an automated system given by God where you go to a divine place and come back with a positive feeling that he has felt at that place. You only need to focus on entering the universal memory. It is tough to access the fearful memories of the universe at a divine place because the universe has only good memories about that place.

Whenever a person goes to divine places, he feels the energy of thousands of people. Because everyone goes with positive energy and gratitude to the divine places. These positive energies create a positive environment at that place. People have a lot of gratitude towards God. People laugh at these places, they thank god, they feel happy there and these memories are also recorded by the universe.

The mind has awesome powers, you just have to use it to accomplish your goal.

Great Thinkers About The Mind's Abilities

Ramanujan Said Everything already exists, we just catch it. You may be shocked after hearing that Albert Einstein discovered the theory of relativity in his dream, and later he worked hard to prove it. Similarly, an Indian mathematician Srinivasan Ramanujan said that his Deity talks to him, and she gives him mathematical formulas. He said that he discovered nothing, his deity whispers formulas in his ear. He first discovered the formula and later proved it.

You may think if everything exists in this universe, then why not stupid people have discovered a great thing yet? This is because stupid people only focus on discovering stupid things. Their mind is occupied with only stupid stuff. Their mind helps them to discover stupidity. You may have seen murderers, thieves, and rapists, they commit crimes very smartly and some of them become smart and masterminds in crimes because they focus on crimes.

Your mind is your servant, it only gives you what you focus on. The mind can give you whatever you focus on. Ideas travel in the form of waves, and that waves can be caught by any focused person. You may have noticed that sometimes an idea comes to your mind and someone else is already doing that. I have personally seen it many times when many business Ideas come to mind and after some days I see them implemented by someone else. This universe already has a solution for every problem. We just have to access the universal consciousness to find our answer.

Unlock Yourself From Inside

The Placebo Effect

In the placebo trial, patients are given fake tablets to treat them. On the other hand, patients believe that they are taking the right medicines to treat their disease, and they will be fine soon. And these placebos work and patients recover as other patients recover who have been given medicines.

After a snake bite, many people die because of heart attacks. Poison rarely becomes the reason for a heart attack. Not always, snake's poison blocks blood circulation in the heart. Maximum times it happens because patients think that a snake has bitten them and their body is poisoned. They believe that this poison will kill them soon. They die out of fear. More people die because of their fear. They could survive and can be treated if they believe in themselves and persist until the medical add, but maximum people lose the battle in the mind. They die because of their fear.

If you believe that you will die then nobody can save you, and if you believe that you can't die then your belief will help you in survival.

A Man in Disaster

In an accident, a person was about to be buried under a stone. He did not have options to choose from. Pushing the stone away was the only hope for him. So he focused on pushing away the stone, and that focus gave him the power to push the stone away. He pushed away from the approximately 1200 kg stone because that stone was about to become his gravestone. He didn't think about the weight of the stone for a single second. He believed that he could, and he did. This is the power of the focus. Many people have proved that humans are limitless. A woman flipped a car to save her baby. There are many examples where people focus because of a situation and show extraordinary courage and power.

We humans have awesome abilities and potential. We can accomplish anything in our life if we use our 100 percent potential. The mind always plays an important role in human life, we can create everything that we can think of. **As Katha Upanishad says "everything that you can imagine, you can bring out it from imagination, a way of making it real already exists, that is why it came into your mind"** it is your duty to find that way to show **it to the world. "It immediately comes into existence in the metaphysical world as you imagine something, You just have to bring it into the physical world.**

Keynotes

- The Human mind can access any memory of the universe, it is so powerful.
- The human mind can sense energy, the human mind can enter into the father's house.
- Humans have the potential of doing extraordinary work, we just have to awaken it with our focus.
- Focus can help us to achieve every goal of our life.

XIII

Direction Of The Energy

To achieve desired results with the help of the power of the subconscious mind, it is necessary to use the energy in the right direction. Energy is the base of every achievement. Nothing can be done without energy. Humans do their daily routine work with this energy. We can use this energy to achieve our goals. Achievers and most successful people accomplish their goals through this energy. We need the right direction of this energy, so we can easily achieve our goals with this energy. So in this lesson, we will discuss the right use of energy and how powerful human energy is.

Global Sports Fans Award

Indian fan Mr. Anil Shah won the award. He is the die heart fan of the most famous cricketer. It would be right if I say he is the worshiper of his favorite cricketer. Before further discussion, it is important to introduce this fan. Why is he special? Anil Shah attended nearly 150 cricket matches played by India, some of these are played in India and some are played internationally. Mr. Anil Shah often traveled by bicycle to reach the venue of the match. He sometimes pedaled his bicycle to cricket-playing venues, as he did to Bangladesh to witness a cricket match in 2007 and to Lahore, Pakistan in 2006. To save money, he sometimes braved travel without tickets in trains to reach venues. When attending cricket matches, he used to paint his body with the tricolor, the colors of the Indian flag, and he used to paint the name of his favorite cricketer on his chest. He used to carry a conch with him and blew the conch to announce the arrival of the National cricket team. Anil used to paint his body on the previous day of a match and used to skip sleep that night to preserve the paint on his body. He cycled for 21 days from Muzaffargarh, Bihar to Mumbai to watch his favorite cricketer play for India against Australia on 28 October 2003 and this was the first tri-series match where he started supporting India by waving the national colors.

In the happy ending of this story, he had been honored by the "Global Sports Fan Award" and His favorite cricketer Hugged him. This is all he achieved in his life.

Is this the purpose of human life: That one day you'll wake up, and one cricketer will hug you and that's it? Don't you think that this man could do better in life if his efforts and actions were in the right direction? If he has used 10% of his energy in improving his life, then we were not introducing him as a poor man or a man who paddles a cycle because of poorness. One can be the biggest fan of someone without wasting such a huge amount of energy in his life. These kinds of extreme fans make cricketers and actors God. They worship them, and they do everything to prove their loyalty towards their Gods. But it is like becoming a slave of your unnecessary desire because someone else is controlling you in that situation. They are not just fans now, they are slaves of that actor or that cricketer. They are wasting their resources, time, and money for free. What will be worse than such a big unproductive person? They got the award for being the best fan, but what can he do with that? His hero is doing his best and earning money and fame for that, but the fan is wasting his life, energy, and resources for that person.

What will be worse than this? Someone has wasted a big part of his life just to be proven a big fan. I mean where it matters. If he has used his energy in the right direction, then he would be able to buy a property next to his hero's house or a cricket team in the IPL.

I feel very sad when I read this type of story. God had created them with a lot of energy to achieve a big goal, but they are wasting it here. They could do much better in their lives, but they wasted their whole life.

Many times he crossed borders just to see his favorite cricketer playing. He could be a better person if he had seen cricket on TV and the rest of the time he could practice cricket. Then he could also become a cricketer if he had used energy in the right direction. He could become the cricket coach because he has enough energy, enough effort, and enough motivation for cricket, but he used it in the wrong direction. He just wasted everything in his life. I want to say that we all owe our energy to the almighty God, our body produces it because God has created our body to produce it. Nobody can say that it's his energy, and he has produced it without the help of nature. It is impossible to produce energy without the help of the almighty God. So it is necessary to use this energy in the right direction. Accomplishing big goals in life that can add value in your life and others' life, will be the right use of energy.

An Actor's Fan

An actor was sentenced to jail for 5 years for his crimes. His die heart fan Walked BARE Feet Till He Came Out Of Jail. He did his every work without shoes for 5 years. He was a rickshaw driver, he had not been wearing shoes for five years because his favorite actor was in jail. Furthermore, the actor was a proven criminal by the court, but his devotee never stopped his worship.

What a shameless devotee that actor has. He shamelessly worships the actor. These types of people don't have any purpose in their life. They are only wasting their energy in the wrong direction and also misleading others. If they had devoted their lives to their goal, they could also become good actors. Even they could be more successful because they have a lot of energy and dedication, but they just wasted it in the wrong direction. If these people use their energy in the right direction, then they can die as rich people, they can die as successful people. If someone doesn't want materialistic things in his life, then he can use his dedication towards salvation, and definitely, he can get salvation. But for that, dedication and energy should be used in the right direction. They can be successful people. I want to quote Bill Gates, **"it is not your fault if you are born as poor, but it is completely your fault if you die as a poor"**

These two examples make it clear that humans don't lack energy, but humans waste energy in the wrong direction. Even the almighty is confused after seeing this kind of misuse of energy. It is unimaginable for our great ancestors.

An Actor's temple

People have made temples of their favorite actors. They worship actors. If you travel across India, you'll find many temples of actors. What a massive misuse of consciousness. What a waste of life, time, devotion, and ethics. These people have found a way to waste divine energy. **These are the people who beg for pennies in a goldmine. Consciousness is a goldmine and energy is gold, and these people are begging pennies in a golden bowl by wasting it.** It proves that people are not poor by lack of resources, rather people are poor by their mindset and misuse of resources. These people are wasting their divine energy on such useless work. A person can achieve his spiritual goal of salvation with this divine energy. A person who uses it in the right direction can achieve everything in life. But these people are wasting this energy in stupidity.

Misuse of Energy

People are wasting their energy in the wrong place. Maybe they want to be famous by doing this kind of stupidity. Or possibly because of a lack of knowledge.

You may have seen people who always talk about girlfriend-boyfriend and other things. Some people only waste their energy in thinking about sex. I agree sex is important, but it doesn't worth your entire energy.

Some porn-addicted people waste their entire day watching porn. Porns don't deserve a single minute because 40% porns are rapes and I am sure nobody wants to be the reason for rape.

Some people are getting expertise in video games, but it isn't worth it. The misuse of energy is disgusting, one should use energy wisely. Energy can destroy a person, or energy can make a person successful. It depends on you what you want from it, it is the same as electricity. If electricity is controlled and used in the right way, it lights up the world but if used to destroy then it becomes disastrous, it can destroy the mountains. It can destroy buildings and even cities in the form of thunder. Energy can do anything. We all have energy in different forms, and these energies can make a huge difference.

Humans Can use limited energy per day, so don't waste it everywhere. As Newton said: **"Energy Can Neither Be Created Nor Destroyed, it Can Be Transformed Only"** So use your energy carefully. For example, Lasers are focused energy and can cut the hardest steel where unfocused energy is useless.

Your focused energy in the right direction can make you successful. Use your energy to do something productive and to achieve your goals. Do meditation, exercise, yoga to focus energy. I know it is not as simple as saying it, it is much harder to implement in life. It is really difficult to focus because we have a fickle mind.

To control a monkey's mind, you just have to withdraw your awareness whenever it goes out of your control. Every time you have to bring it back and focus on your goal. **"your mind can be your best friend if you win it, or it can also be your worst enemy if you lose to it"**.

Use Your Energy To Achieve Your Goal

In college days I used to play cards with friends and I used to take it very seriously whenever we lost in the game. I immediately used to challenge opponents for the next game, I used to challenge them many times, to play again and again until my team won. But after some time I realized that I waste a lot of energy, time, and consciousness in playing cards. Winning cards will not help me to accomplish anything in life. Then I stopped wasting my energy playing cards. I used to play it just for fun and brainstorming but my opponents were still used to teasing us every time we lost to them. They tried to hurt my ego. I analyzed the situations and I stopped playing cards with them because winning in cards was not my goal and it was not helping me to accomplish my goal. I realized that it was a useless battle and I didn't need to win it. I decided to let them call me a loser because their words didn't matter to me and playing cards were not going to help me in any manner. Yes, I am a loser in every worthless battle. I don't play losers' games. I am a loser in useless games. I am a loser of ego.

Use your energy to accomplish your goals. Do not waste energy on everything, don't focus on your desires. One of the biggest mistakes people make, is they run behind every desire and waste their energy to become champions everywhere. **You should invest all of your energy in winning your main battle**, you should invest energy to accomplish your goal. Don't waste your energy fighting every battle. Choose your battle, fight your battle. **Don't participate in every battle, don't fight every battle**. Being a champion everywhere is good. But **losing a battle that doesn't matter, and winning the main battle is awesome. You should not take it on your ego until it doesn't help you to make you successful. It is awesome if you lose somewhere that doesn't matter in the way of accomplishing your goal.** When you take everything on ego and try to become champion everywhere, you waste your precious energy to win useless battles. Focus on your main battle and give your 100% for that.

Ranchod

Lord Krishna could do whatever he wanted, he was the incarnation of Almighty God Vishnu. He did many great works until he was on the earth. But there was also an occasion when Shri Krishna had to leave the battlefield, due to which he was named Ranchod. Lord Krishna ran away from King Kalayavan of Yavana. Because Kalayavan had received a boon from Lord Shankar that neither Chandravanshi nor any Suryavanshi could defeat him in battle. No weapon can kill him, nor can anyone beat him with force. Even despite this, Shri Krishna could kill him, but to respect Lord Shiva's boon he didn't. So Lord Krishna ran away from Kalyavan.

Kalyavan began to consider himself immortal and invincible due to the boon received from Lord Shankar. It seemed that no one could beat him in battle nor kill him. At the behest of Jarasandha, Kalayavan attacked Mathura(Lord Krishna's Capital) with his army. On the other hand, Shri Krishna knew that he did not have to kill Kalayavan with his force, nor with his Sudarshan Chakra. Therefore, he left the battlefield, fled, and reached a dark cave. Where the son of Ikshvaku King Mandhata and King Muchakund of South Kosala was sleeping deeply. (Afterward, he had won the Suras by fighting with the Asuras. He was tired due to war for several consecutive days, so Lord Indra urged him to sleep and also gave him a boon. According to Boon, anyone who wakes them up from sleep will be consumed by burning) Sri Krishna knew the boon received by King Muchkund, so he ran into the cave. Kalyavan followed Shree Krishna to fight with him. Sri Krishna put his Pitambara over Muchkund to confuse Kalayavan. On seeing King Muchkund, Kalayavan felt that it was Shree Krishna and, fearing him, slept in a dark cave. Therefore, considering him as Krishna, he kicked back at King Muchkund. Egoistic Kalyavan Disturbed king Muchkund's sleep as King Muchkund woke up from sleep, Kalayavan was consumed by burning.

Hence, Krishna was named Ranchod(the one who ran away from the battlefield). Lord Krishna gave two messages to the world. First:

"Don't waste energy to make the ego win worthless battles and second, do not participate in others' battles if it is not your battle, then run away from it. Let others fight and win their battles". Even though Lord Krishna could kill Kalyavan only with his wish, he didn't. He had to give the message to the world that one should not waste energy in every battle that doesn't matter. He spread many teachings and did great work, but here Lord Krishna showed that he doesn't have an ego. Lord Krishna was the incarnation of almighty Vishnu, despite this, he didn't take it personally on ego when people called him Ranchod.

Lord Krishna had decided that he would not fight with the Kalyavan because Lord Krishna decided to kill Kalyavan from Muchkund's boon. Lord Krishna had to do great works instead of killing Kalyavan. Lord Krishna had to do many great works for humanity, so he didn't waste his energy on fighting someone else's battle. As we know, Lord Krishna is God and God is the source of every energy, even though he didn't waste it in the wrong place, just to teach a lesson to us. He saved it and did great works for humanity as being within the limits of the human body.

A person loses even after winning a battle where victory doesn't create an impact in life, where victory doesn't match ambition. Don't waste your resources, energy, and time to win a worthless Battle. A person only wastes his energy on such a battle; where he fights the battle just to satisfy his ego and victory doesn't lead him towards his goal. To save energy, a person must avoid situations where chances of wasting energy are high, and it also does not lead towards a goal. In one line, a person who wants to achieve goals in his life should only invest his energy where the investment can help him to accomplish his goal.

Always ask yourself before wasting your energy, is this my battle? Is it worth my energy? You will get answers easily, now you can understand that meeting a cricketer to get hugged by him is not worth your energy. You must have bigger goals, and you have to invest your energy in that. Now you can relate it in every situation and make smart decisions before wasting energy.

Keynotes

- The right direction of energy can make you successful.
- Don't waste your energy to praise other people, use your energy to accomplish your goals.
- It is shameful if we waste our precious energy chasing desires and doing useless work.

XIV

Achieve Your Goals With Positive Thinking

Concept Of Positive Thinking

You may have read books like "Think And Grow Rich", "Power Of Your Subconscious Mind" ETC. These all books have one similar message: you can change your life, or you can have everything in your life by thinking positively. A hidden power works to do everything for you.

Some people also counter these concepts because they have tried these things, and they still have not become millionaires by thinking. Many people counter these things because they believe that success comes with hard work, not by just thinking about success. Different people have different opinions about this.

Many people talk about the power of positive thinking. Many people claim that they have seen the magic of positive thinking. On the other hand, many people try everything that a guru says. Writing goals on paper and all other practices like affirmations, imagination, and feeling the achievement, but they fail to achieve their goal. They imagine and affirm daily, but nothing happens to them.

Many gurus confuse people, one guru says to do this, it will work, it worked for me, so it should also work for you. When people ask them "sir these things are not working" then they blame people for not doing it correctly. You don't have a specific goal, you are not working on it in the right way, you don't have consistency, you don't imagine perfectly, or your childhood conditioning is bad, so it's not working on you.

If you are one of those people who have tried everything to see the magic of the power of positive thinking, affirmation, or power of the subconscious mind, but it never worked on you. If you have followed all instructions of many gurus but nothing happened to you. Then this part of the book will clear all of your doubts. If you are a person who has seen the power of positive thinking, this book will give you more clarity, and you will understand the real power of your mind.

Level Of Energy

We feel very sad when we realize that the power of the subconscious mind is not working on us. We feel bad when we hear that many people have achieved success by using it. We question how and why not me? Why is it not working for us? Many times we get confused about whether this law works or not? So the answer is yes, this law works, and I have used it many times to achieve my goals. Let's understand why the power of the subconscious mind works for some people and why it does not work for some people.

The power of the subconscious mind helps to get a favorable outcome. And for a favorable outcome, a person must have to do work. So it is clear that it is not only about thinking, it is about working and thinking positively. The direction also matters, a person's actions should match with his goal and ambition.

It can also help to achieve a goal, to achieve a goal first you must have a goal.

You are the creator of your life, but not everyone has the same level of energy. That's why the power of the subconscious mind doesn't work for everyone. To use it like prophets and Gandhi, one must have the same level of energy as they had. It is impossible to move a bus with a mobile phone's battery. We need the same level of power supply.

It will be wrong if we compare a person's level 100, versus a person's level 10. A person who has failed to use the power of the subconscious mind, his level is 10, and he has no comparison to the person whose level is 100. "Books on positive thinking" have examples of prophets, Gandhi, and other real-life heroes who had effectively used the power of their subconscious mind and achieved their goals. These books also share stories of some other people who have achieved success in their life through the power of the subconscious mind.

These people were able to use the power of the subconscious mind effectively in their life because they had mastered their minds. They mastered the techniques. **They had increased the level of their energy, they had leveled up their energy**. They had increased their level of energy. This is the main difference between them and a common man.

To level up their energy, they had stabilized thoughts. They did not focus on 1000 things at a time. **They are known to the world because they had one single focus in their life. The world knows them because they achieved their one and main goal in life.** They didn't confuse in thoughts. They had mastered their mind. They had learned to control their thoughts. They had learned to control their desires. They had controlled their mind. That's why they were able to use the power of the subconscious mind effectively.

A person with the energy of level 10 can not be compared with these people because they were legends. But they all were common people before becoming legends, so a common man can also become a legend by following legends' way of success. A common man can also have the same level of energy by following their way. By focussing on one goal at a time, by controlling desires and thoughts.

To increase the level of energy, first, a person needs to preserve the available energy that he has right now. For that, he should not take interest in others' life because he already has a low level of energy, despite this, if he takes interest in others' life then he loses his energy on others. Because energy flows with awareness. If you want to understand the flow of energy, then try a practice for at least 45 days. In this practice, you have to sit down in the meditation pose and imagine that your entire body is made up of purple-colored energy. Try to become aware of your legs and imagine that energy is moving towards your spine from your legs, and energy is stored in your spine, store that energy in your spine, immediately stop the practice, stand up and end the process. After 45 days, you will feel weakness in your legs. Because you have been withdrawing energy from there for 45 days and did not return it. People do similar things when they worry about other people and try to make their situations better just by thinking. Giving consciousness to someone is the costliest and zero effect way to help people. Because with the low level of energy they can't help others just by their low energy, they only lose energy. It means energy wasted without affecting others' life.

We, humans, are emotional, and we try to control others' situations when we see them in trouble and worry about them. This drains energy.

You have to understand that to help others, first, you have to help yourself. First, achieve a higher level of energy, create your great aura, make your dreams true, then try to help others. Great leaders had enough energy to solve everyone's problem, so they solved it. To solve others' problems first you have to become great. Having a low level of energy doesn't mean that it is your drawback, rather it means that you are just starting right now, and it will increase.

There is no reason to worry about other people's problems when you can't solve them. It just drains your energy. Use your limited energy on yourself.

If you use it on yourself, then it will glorify your life. Don't think about shitty things, focus on yourself, don't let this energy flow out of your body for other people. **Don't try to control others' lives because you can't, control your life because you can.** So save this energy, preserve it and your brain powers will help you to accomplish your goal.

Awareness is Important to Achieve Goal

How People Waste Their Awareness

People have their way to waste their awareness. For instance; A friend of mine used to waste his awareness in imagining the future with every girl. Many times, he said that the power of the subconscious mind doesn't work for him. He irritated me with his negative attitude. Frustrated, I asked him, what do you want? You waste your energy in imagining a future with every girl, so how could you expect that you can achieve success? For which girl, your mind should create favorable situations to marry you?

By imagining the future with every girl, you give multiple tasks to your subconscious mind. As a result, **divided attention divides your focus into many thoughts**. The mind distributes the energy in many thoughts, and every thought gets a small part of the energy. Without stability in thoughts, it can't do anything for you. To use the power of the subconscious mind effectively, a person should have a clear vision and a goal that he wants to achieve. He understood my point, and he is now doing good in his life. Now he is successfully running his business.

Many people waste their awareness in thinking about other people. Where some waste their awareness by talking about other people. They talk about the other's family problems. Some waste by bitching about other people.

Many people have a habit of fitting themselves in the loser's situation. Whenever two people fight, some people immediately put themselves in the situation and present opinions. They say words like, If I were at the place of this person, then I would do this. Whenever a person tells them about him, they immediately answer that if I would be at your place, then I did things in a better way.

These are all cheap ways of wasting awareness. Always remember where awareness goes, energy flows. Remember the law, energy neither be created nor destroyed humans have limited energy in their bodies. We have to preserve energy by preserving our awareness.

Be Aware While Using Power

If you know about the power of the subconscious mind then you must know that it is 50% about imagination, by imagining our goal we emit energy on that goal and this energy helps us to accomplish that goal. People always waste their awareness in imagining useless thoughts. What can the "power of the subconscious mind" attract to a person who has thousands of thoughts and imaginations at a time? Humans have limited energy, and energy flows with awareness. Where awareness goes, energy flows. Never let your awareness go in the wrong direction. Keep only those thoughts in your mind that do not waste your awareness. Again, remember the law, energy neither be created nor be destroyed. So you have only 100% energy. You have to use it to make things happen in your life that you imagine. Your imagination power helps you to give you everything that you want in life.

Now if a person is busy imagining himself in the place of other people then this law will lead him in that person's place. How can a Casanova expect success in life by imagining sex for the whole day? By putting entire energy into sex, nobody should expect success. He can only run after sex, he has limited himself only to sex. He has chosen sex as his limit.

Suppose a person has 100% energy daily, and he has 100 thoughts. He is a daydreamer. Then this energy will be divided into 100 thoughts by the mind. As a result, each thought will have 1 percent energy. This one percent is not enough to achieve a goal. This one percent energy will only give a 1% result, every thought will be wasted.

We have discussed before that humans have a fickle mind and it is impossible to stop thoughts, but it is possible to not waste awareness on those thoughts. Let the useless thoughts come and go out. Do not waste awareness on them by going deep. Do not waste energy in imagining useless thoughts. Discontinue every useless thought. Whenever a useless thought comes into mind, you just have to ignore that thought. Do not let it steal your awareness. Do not dwell in that thought. You just have to withdraw your awareness from these kinds of thoughts as soon as possible. This is how you can preserve your energy. Invest this energy to imagine your goal and success. Invest this energy to think about something productive.

If you use your energy only on a few things, then definitely this energy will make it happen.

If you give 1000 orders to your brain at a time, then what do you expect to be true? You have given him many orders, you have already wasted energy by dividing it among many thoughts. Big goals need a larger amount of energy. But many orders have already drained your energy. As a result, you will not have sufficient energy to achieve a goal.

The only solution is, you can use your energy only to achieve your goal, (which means you don't give a damn to other things). If you use your energy only on a few things, then this will help you to achieve it.

Everyone Is An Achiever (Where He Focuses)

Some young boys spend their whole day thinking about girls. As a result, they chase girls, they invent new ways to impress girls, they explore new things about girls and some boys even know more about girls than girls. These boys are also discovering, they are also geniuses in their fields. They can have many girlfriends(But always remember they will only attract girls of their type who have the same level of energy and awareness because to attract great, greater energy is needed) We cannot call them unsuccessful. Because they are successful in their interests. They are achieving what they want to achieve. Their brain is also working in a direction where they want to use it. You achieve what you focus on. **"Focus leads you towards your Aim, it doesn't matter your Aim at a goal, or your aim at a piece of shit" focus doesn't care about it, it only gives you what you want. Focus does not have the capability of thinking.**

In their 60s they can be called unsuccessful because they may not have money at that time. But they would have been successful in their priority, they would have achieved success in impressing many girls. Their hard work would have paid them, because they had spent time in the gym to build a body just to impress girls, and they have done it successfully. They would have achieved success in their interest. Maybe this is the success in Casanova's eyes. Rich and self-made people could be the biggest losers in their eyes.

Everyone achieves their goal **"for mind success is measured by the accomplishments of goals, priorities that a person has set to the mind".** For the mind, it doesn't matter what a person has achieved. The mind only recognizes the achievements. If a person feels unsuccessful in his 60s because of a lack of money. Then this will be the result of his 20s priorities. Give the task to your brain that can make you successful. Give it the right direction and right goal. It will achieve it.

Lord Krishna says **"You will undoubtedly reach where you want to go, In the end, people go where they focus".** It means you will achieve success in your goal. You will undoubtedly achieve your goal if you focus enough. Your mind will give you everything that you want. In other words, you may say that the only ending is a success, there is nothing like a failure, only quitter and winners.

Use, Full Energy

Use your energy to accomplish your goal. Your goal needs your 100% energy. Stay focused to achieve your goals. Do not worry about the world. Never let your energy go out of you. Use the power of your subconscious mind to accomplish your goal. Imagine the accomplishment of your goal daily. Think about that goal. Take action to achieve that goal. Do not let other people drain your energy. Control your awareness.

Keynotes

- Positive thinking can help you to accomplish any goal.
- Increase your level of energy.
- We all have the same source of energy, and we all can increase the level of our energy...
- You can achieve everything in your life if you focus enough.
- Everyone achieves what he focuses on, focus always wins
- Be aware of using the power of the subconscious mind.
- Do not waste your awareness on other people.

XV
Take Control

Control yourself

What do you want to do by using the power of the subconscious mind? The obvious answer is to control your life. To control your life, you need to control your energy. Control starts with the mind. If you can control your mind and body, then you can think about controlling your life.

You May have heard about the connection between Billionaire Steve Jobs and Baba Neem Karoli. Steve Jobs had said that he was blessed by Baba Neem Karoli's divine powers. He had deep faith in Baba Neem Karoli which is why the second time Mark Zuckerberg visited with Steve Jobs to the divine place of Baba Neem Karoli.

Many sages have the power to control other people's lives because they have so much energy. Have you ever thought about how Maharishis' (great sages)' boon becomes true? Answer: they have learned how to control their energy, and they don't waste it, Maharishis don't even waste their energy to curse an enemy. They always preserve energy. They continuously increase the level of their energy by meditating, controlling thoughts, desires, self-control, and by Yoga.

In ancient India, Rishi Munis used to go into caves and on mountains to do Tapasya and Dhyan(meditation) to avoid distractions and interruption. As a result, they used to become more powerful. They had better control over every circumstance. They had become perfect, and that's why they had so much power in their words. If they had blessed someone to be successful, then definitely he would become successful. This is called Maharishi's boon. But not every sage had the same power; it also depends on the level of sage's energy.

Indians have a ritual of touching the feet of every respected and wise person. In return, they receive blessings. Ancient Indians knew the power of blessings, so they added them to their culture. They added it in culture to take blessings by touching the feet of elder people. This process is giving respect and receiving blessings, here receivings is a thousand times more than giving. They knew that wise man's blessings are really powerful, and these blessings can add value to their life. Blessing can help them live happy life. In the modern world affirmations are self blessings, but they are not the same thing.

Can Anyone Stop Your Growth?

This question is very obvious: can a person do anything wrong with other people with his negative thinking? If positive thinking works, then why not negative? If blessings work, then why not curse? The answer is yes if a person has achieved full control of his mind, has a high level of energy, and has learned to control energy then he can, but it needs a lot of energy. This sometimes can cost his entire life's energy. That is why sages avoid cursing people. This can cost a sage his entire life's asceticism. Negative thoughts take more energy and emit weaker frequencies. These frequencies are 1000 times weaker than a positive thoughts' frequency, so for a common man, it is near to impossible to affect other people's lives with negative thoughts. And a person who has the ultimate level of energy and achieved awesome control over it. He is not going to waste his energy to impact other people's lives because he requires this energy for him, and he knows its value. He never interferes in others' lives. That was the first step of his growth.

A person who does not have an energy level equal to the sages' negative thinking can only harm himself. His negative thoughts and imagination do not work on other people. Because everyone has their consciousness and energy. Your aura is sufficient to protect you from other people's negative energy. Two energies will crash, and your energy will win because positive energy is 1000 times stronger than negative energy.

But it doesn't mean that you have to be surrounded by negative people, emotions are contagious and negative emotions create negative energy around you. If you are surrounded by negative people then your thoughts also affect and your thinking becomes negative.

A person who has a low level of energy should never try to control other people's life. Because it is a total wastage of energy. And a person who believes that his energy level is high should also focus on his goals instead of trying to control other people's lives. **"Lord Krishna says in the Geeta "every human is free, no one controls his life, even God himself does not interfere in the people's life.**

Control Your Life

You do not have to go to caves or on Everest peak and do austerity. You just have to use your energy effectively to achieve your goal.

The power of the subconscious mind works in a proportion of ability to control energy. Only controlled energy can do miracles for you, uncontrolled energy will be wasted. If you waste it everywhere, then this cannot perform miracles for you.

If you do not know where your energy is going, then you can't control it. So first you need to know the direction of your energy. To know the direction of energy, you should observe your thinking for the whole day. Do you waste energy in anger? Or you waste your energy thinking about other people. What are your thoughts? First, become an observer, then try to control it. Try to control it by controlling your mind and body. We have already discussed some ways to control our minds. Now we will discuss some ways to control the body to preserve energy and use that in the right direction.

The one who cannot control their body, how can he control his circumstances? Your mind learns everything by practicing. If you practice controlling your body and habits, the mind learns to control. The more you practice control, the more your mind becomes expert.

For example: If you go to the gym and do exercise daily as a result, your body gets stronger. If you practice lifting the weight, then your capacity of lifting weight increases. Your body does not say that I only lift the instruments of the gym, I don't lift anything else. Similarly, when you practice controlling your body, your mind becomes more powerful in controlling. It learns how to control the body and desire. How to control anger and your mood. So try to learn control with small things. If you fail then don't rush because by rushing you send negative messages to your brain about it. So first thing, never rush. Try to control yourself when you want to eat junk foods, try to control your body when you want to smoke, control yourself when you want to watch porn. Take it as a challenge of controlling yourself.

You may think what will happen by doing this?

The controlling power of your mind will be stronger as you continue to practice control, your power of control grows, and it helps you to control your subconscious mind. This power of control will help you to control your life. By learning to control your body, desire, and lust you learn to control, and it helps you to control your subconscious mind. Your controlled subconscious mind can control your energy, and your energy can control your circumstances. The controlling level grows, it grows until it becomes able to control your life and its circumstances.

It gives you the freedom to choose where your energy should go. Once you control your mind and energy, you become a master in controlling your life.

Thinking about useless things is a waste of energy. One should immediately withdraw his energy from useless thought to stop it from using a huge part of his energy. Suppose a thought comes to your mind about fighting a person or anything else like fiction movies. It is not relevant to your goal, you should not waste your time and energy on enjoying that moment in your mind, rather you should immediately control your mind and withdraw your awareness from that thought. Do not go deep on that thought.

Sexual Energy

In ancient India, Bhrahamacharya was the most important concept for a sage. A Brahmachari is a person who does not do sex and does even not think about sex. Every sage has to be Bhramachari (Pure virgin). There are many benefits mentioned of Brahmacharya in the great Vedic scriptures. A sage's journey is incomplete without the Brahmacharya. In the case of accomplishing a pure divine heart, Brahmacharya is essential for the sages. Now I am going to explain the science behind Brahmacharya. Foremost it is not about saving your sperm, many people misunderstand that they have to save sperm for a better life. Many people have explained it incorrectly. It is not about preserving the sperm. It is about preserving energy because sex takes a lot of energy. Sperm will not give a boost to your body or ejaculation will not weaken your body. Rather it will preserve your energy because sperm has the power of creation that is why it takes a lot of energy to form sperm. A complete Brahmchari saves energy both physically and mentally. He even doesn't think about sex to save his 100% sexual energy. He doesn't even waste the energy of creation in imagining sex. If one controls his sexual activities, energy saved from the formation of sperm can be used to accomplish the goal. This energy is so strong because it is the energy of creation. If someone uses it in the right direction, then this can give awesome results. It is the most powerful energy. Transmutation of this energy is highly beneficial.

Power Of Creation

You need the energy to accomplish your goal. If your goal is something that doesn't exist in the materialistic world right now. Then sexual energy can help you a lot to create it because sexual energy has the power of creation. According to great ancient Vedas, **"deities help us to do everything by giving us their powers"**. They do it to serve the almighty Vishnu's integral part, that stays in our body that is our soul, yes our soul is an integral part of the almighty god. All the other deities are representatives of Vishnu's powers, we call them by different names. **Deva Ganesh is the god of good luck, wiseness, fame, and auspiciousness so his power helps us to become wise. (According to Vedas, one who wants to be wiser should worship Ganesha, should follow Ganesha's Way).** He is always remembered first on every auspicious occasion because he clears obstacles. Lord Indira gives his powers to the heart. **Brahma dev is the God of creation, he is the representative of the power of creation of almighty God Vishnu. Brahma has created the universe, he has created every existence of the universe. So he has the power of creation. His every creation has this power.** You also have the power of creation on your level. Yes, you also have this. You can use this power to transform your life. Because this power comes from the same source of power which created the universe. I believe that your goal is not as big as creating a separate universe for you. You just have to accomplish your goal with the help of this power. To accomplish your goal, your power of creation is enough for you. **You want something that is already created by the god of creation, and you just have to make it yours. Isn't it super easy?** Because you don't have to create it, you just have to use your energy to make it yours. **Lord Krishna says in Geeta "I created everything".** A human can also create everything in this universe with his power of creation(like many people did in history, Martin Cooper invented the mobile phone, first, he had only thought about it then he worked hard to create it in reality. Similarly, many people have made their thoughts a reality, they all did it with the power of creation). Every human has this power of creation, whether it is a girl or a boy.

So according to the great Vedas, we all have the power of creation. That is why we humans are called creators. It is up to you where you use this power. A person who only uses the power of creation just to satisfy his sexual desire is similar to a dog. Dogs also use their power of creation just to do sex. We do not have a power level similar to the god of creation. We can not create a universe with our power, but we have enough to create our life. We have enough to create anything in this universe. We have more than enough to accomplish our goals. We just have to use this power of creation to accomplish our goals. We can create everything in our life with this power. But this power is useless if it is only used to do sex. We need to use this power to accomplish goals. We need to learn to control it.

Sexual Desire

Sexual desire is the most powerful desire in humans. That is why Yogis start their journey by controlling sexual desire. They take an oath to follow Brahmacharya varat. They have bigger goals and for that, they need this energy. They have goals beyond a common man's imagination. They have spiritual goals. They consider the physical world as useless and Maya. They do not take any interest in this materialistic world and its race. They don't want anything in this world, not fame, name, money, power, and sex, nothing. They consider these things as cheap things. Their goals are beyond these things. They have much bigger goals, and they achieve those goals by controlling their sexual energy and desires.

When we try to control our sexual desire, we preserve energy plus learn control on sexual energy. Why is controlling sexual desire so important? Because this desire is the most difficult desire to control. If someone successfully controls it, then it can give him tremendous results. In the book Think and grow rich, author Napoleon Hill has explained it as "Sexual Transmutation".

Swami Vivekananda had awesome control over his sexual desire. That is why Swami Vivekananda was the most influential person of his era. He was the wisest man. His goal was different. He did awesome work in the spirituality field. He did achieve everything that he wanted to achieve in his life.

The right use of this energy is not difficult. Try these techniques for 45 days, and you will see awesome results. It can transform your life. The procedure is very simple. First, you just have to control your body, do not masturbate, if married, do sex only with your spouse at least in the gape of 15 days. Second, you have to control your desire, do not watch porn, and do not imagine sex. If sexual thought comes into your mind, imagine your success and goal immediately. Feel the appreciation of your dearest one. Think about the success and feeling that you will feel after achieving the goal.

You have to preserve energy in two places. Once you have to save energy directly in your body. Where you control your sexual activities.

Second, you have to avoid sexual thoughts, porn, and talking about sex.

A person who successfully controls his body and preserves the energy of creation, but always imagines sex pleasures and sex. He can never use this energy to accomplish his goals because he is preserving energy at the physical level and wasting it on a mental level. It is not only physical. After controlling sexual energy, you can control the power of creation. The power of creation can make it so easy to accomplish your goal.

Imagination

You can use the power of imagination to control your mind, and your controlled mind can control your life. Now you may be confused that this person was saying that don't waste awareness in imagining useless thoughts, but now he is saying that use the power of imagination to control your mind.

There is a huge difference between thinking about random thoughts and thinking about what you want to think. When you dwell on random thoughts, then your random thoughts win your awareness. But when you imagine what you want to imagine, then you win, because your mind is thinking according to you. You control your awareness. You train your mind to imagine according to you. You control your imaginations. You force your mind to think what you want to think. In the first few weeks, you may feel difficulty imagining what you want to imagine, but after some days you will master your imagination. This will be the time when you will have good control over your mind.

Once your mind imagines according to you then your mind will be your slave, a person who can't control it is the slave of the mind. This is the simplest way to control your mind. This will help you to achieve your goal because when you think about anything your mind emits waves and these waves can help you to achieve your goal. This wave works for you. You will master this technique easily if you practice imagination daily.

You may have heard that the subconscious mind doesn't know how to discriminate between imagination and reality. I have an appropriate example of it when a man Imagine sex he got aroused. His sexual organ immediately got an erection. This is because the subconscious mind doesn't know that this is just an imagination, and it is not real. The subconscious mind believes that imagination is real, and he has to prepare the body for sex. Similarly, it affects your life. It emits waves and these waves work to convert imagination into reality. When you daily imagine the same goal, your brain emits the same waves daily and this wave tries to show you results. To emit strong waves, all processes written in this book must be followed.

A person should imagine that he has already achieved his goal. He should imagine it daily because when your mind emits the same waves daily then he will be practiced enough to emit stronger waves and these stronger waves can create favorable circumstances to achieve the goal. By imagining success in the same goal daily, your mind learns to emit the same waves more strongly. Because it has practiced for it.

Subconscious Mind Never Sleeps

Your subconscious mind never sleeps, takes rest, or takes a break because it controls all vital processes and functions of the body. For instance, the subconscious mind controls heartbeat, blood circulation, regulates digestion and elimination. In sleep, your conscious mind sleeps when you sleep while the subconscious mind stays fully awake.

The subconscious mind does not know the difference between reality and imagination. The conscious mind differentiates between reality and imagination. So whenever a person sleeps and sees horror dreams, he feels scared and his heartbeat increases at the same as it increases when a person fears in real life. He feels every pressure and fear in the dreams because the innocent subconscious mind believes that he is in danger, in reality, so he raises the heartbeat and other processes.

Boys who have faced nightfall know it very well. Similarly, many girls can reach orgasm by just imagining sex. So it is easy to understand that reality starts with imagination. By imagining things, our mind sends energy to that part of the body. The Subconscious mind believes in imagination and dreams to be true. In dreams, our conscious mind gets asleep, so it does not tell the difference between a dream and reality to the subconscious mind. At that time, If a person does sex in his dreams, the subconscious mind believes it to be true and the person ejaculates in the dream. The person was doing sex in dreams, but he saw results in reality because he couldn't differentiate. So this is how imaginations concentrate energy and shows result in the physical world. You can accomplish everything in the physical world if you use it efficiently.

Feeling Of The Achievement

Why is it important to feel the achievement in the imagination process? To understand it, we need to understand two concepts. **The first is practice and the second is a habit.**

Practice

Do you know how vaccines work? You may have heard about some vaccines that contain inactive viruses. These vaccines work on a principle where inactive viruses are injected into the body(of course it takes a lot of research and experimentation to make it safe for humans). In some vaccines where research shows that even an inactive virus can be dangerous scientists pick a similar but less harmful and non-dead virus, put it in the vaccine, and give the dose to the human. In this process, science uses the power of the human subconscious mind to defeat the virus. In this process, an inactive virus is injected into the body as a reaction mind sends its fighters to fight with this unfamiliar virus. The fighters easily learn to defeat the virus because it was an inactive virus. In the second dose of the vaccine, the human immune system practices and checks its skills to fight against the virus. After enough practice, the immune system becomes an expert in killing the virus and develops immunity against the virus. Once the immune system learns to defeat the inactive virus, then the mind collects the data about the battle and makes our body's defense system stronger. So next time, whenever a similar virus enters the body, the immune system immediately kills it because it has enough immunity against it. Our mind only needs data once, and it prepares everything better for the next time. It was prepared for it. The human mind deals better and the chances of winning become more if it has prepared before starting a real battle. No doubt our mind can defeat any virus in its first attempt, but it does it better with practice. He defeats more effectively, with minimum damage, if the mind practiced it before. Feeling success in the process of imagination is the same process as this.

So here we can understand that our mind can do better work if we help it to practice.

Feeling about the achievement of your goal is a practice. It prepares the subconscious mind for success. It clears doubts of the subconscious mind that is related to the goal. It helps the subconscious mind to feel successful. It makes it easier for the subconscious mind to accomplish the goal in reality. It integrates the energy of emotion with the energy of imagination, and your body emits more energy to achieve your goal. The energy of emotions is powerful.

Habit

Second is the habit: our brain tends to repeat habits. A smoker doesn't need to be reminded that he has to smoke. His body automatically tells him that he needs to smoke. He feels incomplete or missing something if he doesn't smoke. We tend to repeat the habit so when a human feels and imagines his achievements daily, it becomes his habit, by imagining success, it becomes a habit. The subconscious mind works with its full power to make it real because it feels good to repeat habits. A habitual person's mind craves for goals as an addicted crave smoking. The subconscious mind does its full efforts to make it happen because it is a habit now. So feel the success to make it happen.

Power Of Emotions

Jonathan Goodwin flipped a car by imagining his daughter under the car. American stuntman Jonathan Goodwin was impressed by the hidden powers of the subconscious mind. He wanted to explore it. He had watched a story on TV, where a woman flipped a car to save her daughter. This story impressed Jonathan, so he decided to explore his power of emotions to save his daughter. He imagined his daughter under the car, and to save her he had to flip the car.

He felt the depth of his love towards his daughter and once he convinced his mind that his daughter is under the car in reality, then he attempted a trial to flip the car, and he successfully flipped the car. He proved that this power was within him. He awakened it with his imaginations plus emotions. His feelings played an important role to awaken the hidden power in himself. As we know, energy is the most essential thing to achieve a goal. So by this way, we can put more energy into work.

Heart's Role

The human heart produces stronger energy than the human mind. That is why it is essential to include the heart in this process. The first step of including the heart is already completed. When we feel high, our heart generates high energy. Our heart has the energy to do things more efficiently. The heart is powerful, it has power and the mind is smart and knows how and where to use power. So this combination is crucial.

Here I have an effective technique to get more effective results. First, sit down in the meditation pose. Put the left leg on the right leg or vice versa. Close your eyes, you can also play meditation music. Imagine energy is flowing through your whole body. The color of energy is purple. This energy is everywhere in your body. Now focus on the energy of your heart. Now imagine this energy is flowing from your heart to your mind through your spine. It goes to the end of the spine. Now imagine your goal, imagine you have achieved it with the help of this energy. In the starting days, you will feel nothing, but by the time you realize that your heart beats differently when you imagine your goal. You will notice that it beats in the same way as it beats when you see your love. Your heart rate increases whenever you think about your goal. Your heart beats differently whenever you think about your goal. This is because your heart generates more energy to help you to accomplish your goal. It will send a huge amount of energy to achieve your goal. You will see good and fast results if you try this technique without missing a single day. This practice requires consistency and dedication.

Warning

We need energy in every aspect of life. We require energy to achieve goals in life. Imaginations and techniques work well, but actions are most important to achieve your goal. Goals need dedication. A person who has a clear vision and organized planning can achieve his goal with these techniques. People who do not have any goal or vision can achieve nothing in their life. One day they imagine the car and the next day they imagine a plane. These people achieve nothing in their life. Success has a step-by-step process, you have to follow every step to be successful. As I mentioned, the power of the subconscious mind is all about good outcomes. A person who doesn't take any action, can't have an outcome. A student can never pass an exam without attempting the exam. **A student can never top in exams just by giving exams and thinking about positive results,** he has to study for that. Because the power of the subconscious mind is not about gambling. It brings opportunities to you, but you must grab the opportunity. It is a science, and it works with a system. You have understood the concept of energy, and you know very well how energy can help you to achieve your goal. For instance, energy is flowing through the wire but if there is no bulb then how can that energy light the room? A system is required to light the room. Similarly, the subconscious mind needs a proper structure to work. It is a step-by-step process. You have to follow a full process to achieve your goal. The full process includes learning, knowledge, organized planning, work, efforts, persistence, and attitude. You will always have what you deserve. You have to become the most deserving person. If you are deserving then soon you will have what you deserve. Then, these techniques guarantee success. Thousands of people have achieved their goals with these techniques, but they all worked for their goals. This book is not about fictional stories, this book is about making you successful.

This book aims to help you to achieve your goal. This book is for the winner who believes in only one happy ending that is a success. This book is for action takers. Energy and subconscious mind work for you if you work for your goal. This both works in a combination, it doesn't work without one.

Keynotes

- If you want to control your life, start with controlling your body, habit, and emotions.
- Sexual energy is the most powerful energy in the human body, a human can achieve everything with this energy if he uses it in the right direction.
- To use sexual energy in the right direction, a person must avoid sexual thoughts because it wastes energy too.
- The mind produces energy, so it is important to control energy within the mind.
- Imagination and feeling of achievement include a person's energy towards his goal.
- You have the power of creation, you can use it to create a better life for you.
- Your heart generates stronger energy, you can use it to achieve everything in your life.
- To achieve anything from the power of the subconscious mind, you need to work in the right direction.

Part Four

PRODUCTIVITY AND TIME MANAGEMENT TO ACHIEVE GOALS

XVI
Productivity To Achieve Goal

To achieve goals in life, Productivity is very essential. To be productive, we need to use time effectively. Time is the most essential factor in human life because we all have a limited amount of time in our life. Everyone has 24 hours in a day, not even billionaires have 48 hours in a day. Even billions of dollars can not buy a single second. Time is the most expensive thing. We all have the same time. Maximum output in a limited time is called productivity. The difference is how we manage it and how much output we get from it. We need to use our productive time to get the most productive output from it.

Our time is limited, so **we have to do more in less time**. This is what achievers do to achieve their goals. They do more in less time, therefore they are called productive people. We need productivity to achieve more in less time.

Productivity has a simple definition: **doing more work with higher accuracy in the right direction in less time is called productivity.** This work should be done in the right direction and this work should increase the level of the person. **A work that gives you growth, helps you to accomplish your goal is called productive work.** We only have to focus on the goal, not on desires. Use productivity to achieve the goals in our life.

Productive Time

What is productive time? Productive time is the time when a person feels so focused and fresh. Everyone has a time when he can focus more. At productive times, a person's mind is more active than at any other time. At productive times, new ideas come into a person's mind. At productive times, the person feels energetic. His heart says that he can achieve everything in his life. A person's energy stays at its peak at his productive time. This high energy helps a person to work more efficiently and with perfection. And this perfection can help him to achieve his goal. The right use of productive time is really important to achieve goals.

Best Use of Productive Time

Your productive hours must be used to work towards your goal. It should not be wasted to make changes in others' lives. It should be only your time. Your Priority should be your goal at a productive time. Because at this time you can work more efficiently to achieve your goal.

Productive time is all about mental productivity, don't confuse it with your fitness goal. Always use this time when your mental abilities can be used, do not waste this time in the gym to build muscles. You can go to the gym in unproductive time because the gym doesn't need your productive time. Use it to do productive work only. Use this time to do something to accomplish your goal.

Find Your Productive Time

Everyone should find their productive time of the day. Every day, humans have a time when they feel most productive. People who wake up in the early morning by choice are usually considered morning people. And people who stay awake late nights are usually night people. Some people are productive at both times. These people can work productively at both times. Everyone has a productive time in a day. Some people are night people and some are morning people. Most of the people belong to these two categories. Some people also can be productive at the time of the day. So find your productive time and use it well. To improve your life, use this time and its energy to achieve your goals.

Here I have some ways to find your productive time.

- To know about your productive hours, try to do work in random hours. Check progress, collect data, check-in at which time you were most productive, at which time you did most of your work and your output was the most.
- In which hours you did not get bored by working.
- Try to solve mathematical problems at the time of observation, in which time you were able to solve problems easily and in less time.
- Try to do the toughest work and observe it, collect data and note down your progress.
- Try doing your most important piece of work for the day as soon as you get into work for a couple of weeks and see how that feels.

Finding your productive time doesn't mean you just have to work only in productive time. You just have to use the productive time to do more in less time. You have to use the productive time to do the most critical and urgent work. You have to use your productive time to achieve your goal.

Increase Your Productivity

As we have discussed before, productivity is important to achieve goals. The use of productive time is critical to achieving goals. Because it can give more in less time, therefore, it saves your time. No one can buy more time, but everyone can do more in less time if they use productive time efficiently. We have already understood that the right use of productive time is critical, now we will discuss some techniques to increase our productivity, so we can increase our productive time. Because more productivity means more opportunities to achieve goals. Opportunities must be grabbed to be successful. So there is a need to increase productivity. Because our time is limited, we have to achieve our goals in this limited time. Without energy and productivity, we can't do work efficiently. So we will discuss how to increase productivity. How to convert unproductive hours to productive hours.

Meditation

Meditation is a best practice to increase productivity. One should start the day by meditating for a few minutes. It is no more a hidden secret that meditation helps a person to be productive. Meditation increases the efficiency of a person, and it also helps to calm the mind. Calming the mind can never be a waste of time. A calmed mind can focus more. Meditation is the secret key to increasing productivity. Meditation results don't take years to show the results. It increases productivity immediately because it is directly related to the mind.

To do meditation you have to sit down on the floor on a soft mat, keep your spine straight and put your left leg on the right leg. After that, put your right hand on your left hand, place it on your lap. Close your eyes and be aware of your surroundings. (Keep your mind active because meditation is an active process. Thinking about nothing and trying to practice meditation by laying on the bed is not meditation. Because there is a difference between meditation and sleeping. Meditation is an active process while lying in a bed and trying to do meditation is similar to trying to sleep). To increase productivity, focus on your goal while doing meditation (you may also focus on your breath). Focus on the importance of the goal. Aware of the need to achieve the goal. Because meditation is all about the focus at a point. Because of focusing on your goal, your mind realizes the importance of the goal. That is why you are focusing on this, so your mind will generate energy. You will feel energetic instantly. This special energy will make you more productive. Your mind will be focused on your goal. With this increased energy, you can work more efficiently and productively. Your output will be maximum.

Yoga And Pranayama

Why didn't I talk about the gym? Because the gym is more about your physical body. To do something productive, you have to nurture your body and mind both. Yoga and pranayama are about setting a balance between body and mind. The balance between body and mind is important to be productive. Yoga has unlimited health and mental benefits, if I discuss all of them then this book will not be enough to cover them. However, Some benefits are here: it helps to stimulate the mind, it also sets a balance between the mind and body, it helps to control emotions, it helps to control bad habits, it also gives good health, it can cure many diseases, it has many health benefits, it sharpens the brain. It also has awesome spiritual benefits. Spirituality also increases the productivity of the person.

Yoga

Let's discuss how Yoga increases productivity. Yoga means addition (plus) that is why it is called yoga because it adds value to your life. It can also add more productivity in life. It has many ways to give energy to a person. To increase productivity, Yoga increases the concentration power of the person. A concentrated person can do everything more efficiently. A concentrated person does more work in less time, effectively. Practicing yoga not only calms your mind but gives you a great energy boost on the inside. Performing yoga in your workplace has proven benefits within as well as beyond work-life to be filled with energy, concentration, and peace. Work, which is done with concentration, can give awesome results.

Yoga helps to avoid stress and anxiety. A person who does not have stress and anxiety will never feel stress and anxiety if he develops a habit of doing regular yoga. Stress, anxiety, and tension kill a person's productivity. These all drain a person's productivity, so Yoga and Pranayam help to avoid these all. So a person without stress, tension, and anxiety can do more work efficiently. His brain stays active all the time and works better, so naturally, it increases the person's productivity.

Pranayama

There is a difference between yoga and pranayama. The practice of pranayama involves breathing exercises and patterns. You purposely inhale, exhale, and hold your breath in a specific sequence. In yoga, you practice physical postures and asanas. Where yoga is about the body postures and Asana, Pranayama is about breathing and its ways. It is more about controlling and regulating the breath. It is more about the chakras of the body. Pranayama is more helpful in spiritual journeys.

Pranayama is very useful and the easiest way to increase productivity. Pranayama is more about the inside of the body, where Yoga focuses on the inside and outside equally. Pranayama focuses more on the inside. Pranayama works more on the heart and brain. The heart and the brain are the most important parts of the body to increase productivity.

Pranayama increases the heart rate, which is also good for heart health. When a person starts doing pranayama he develops patience by sitting down. With this patience, he starts developing better control of his breathing and heart. As a result, he starts to learn to control his body. A person who has better control over his body and desire becomes a more productive person.

Distraction is one of the main reasons for unproductivity. Unproductive people feel distracted while doing work, and they follow their distractions. So you can get rid of distractions with the help of Pranayama. Pranayama helps a person to set a good combination between the heart and brain. When the brain and heart have a better combination, a person does not face distractions in doing work. So this combination increases his productivity.

It is mentioned in ancient Vedic scriptures that Pranayama, especially Kapalbharti and Bhastrika Pranayama, is helpful to control the Kundalini. It helps to awaken Kundalini Shakti. Kundalini Shakti stays in the Muladhara Chakra in the human body. Mainly, it controls sexual desire in the human body. By controlling the Kundalini you can also control your sexual desires. It means sexual desires will rarely distract you. If you successfully control this desire, then you will be more productive. You control your desire, it can not control you and not distract you while doing work. So you will be able to work more efficiently, and you will be able to do more in less time.

So this is how Yoga and Pranayama can help you a lot to increase your productivity. Yoga and Pranayama help you to become more productive!

Food

Some special foods increase a person's productivity. Some foods drain productivity.

Usually, maximum fruits increase productivity. Apple, banana, berries, avocados, etc. These fruits are often easy to digest, and they have a lot of vitamins and proteins. So that is how they support the brain, and a healthy brain has more productivity. Dry fruits like almonds and cashews are also good for the brain, these fruits also boost the brain. These fruits have long-lasting benefits to the brain, so one must take these fruits.

Instant Boosters

Drinking a cup of tea also gives an instant boost. Tea has caffeine and L-theanine that increase alertness and focus of the brain. It works more efficiently if your body is not tea habitual. Drinking tea continuously will not increase productivity because tea does not have enough nutrients to nourish the brain. It does not have enough vitamins and proteins to benefit your brain for the long term. So do not go for it for long-lasting benefits. It does not have any long-lasting benefits to your brain. Go for it only for an instant boost if you feel lazy and distracted.

Water

The Largest component of our brain is water. As such, even slight dehydration can cause fatigue, headaches, lack of mental clarity, stress, and sleep issues. So obviously we need to keep ourselves hydrated. To use our brain efficiently. Every doctor says to drink water properly and avoid dehydration, but we all ignore it. But to increase productivity, you have to drink water properly. So whenever you feel unproductive and less concentrated, dehydration can be the cause. So always drink water properly to stay productive.

Foods That Drains Productivity

Junk foods are on the top of the list. Junk foods drain your productivity instantly. These foods also have bad effects on the body and brain. These foods can affect cognitive function. These foods take more energy to digest as a result the brain's energy is wasted to digest unhealthy food. After wasting a lot of energy, it does not give good proteins and vitamins to the brain. "It is a situation like working more and paid less" disappoints the brain. These foods are not good for productive people. I have listed some foods below that should be avoided by a productive person.

- Artificial sweeteners
- Fast Food
- Fried foods
- Processed and convenience foods
- Very salty foods

- Processed Proteins

To stay productive, you should also avoid eating heavy, and heavy foods. After eating heavy food, your maximum energy gets drained in the digestion process. The same happens with foods that are heavy to digest. Foods that are heavy to digest also use more energy to be digested and use most of the brain's energy.

At the time of evolution, the main reason for the human brain's growth was the fire. Because of the fire, we were able to cook our food and that is why our food became easy to digest. The human body started to save a lot of energy that would be used in the process of digestion. That saved energy worked on our brain development. This is how our brain developed.

So it is clear that humans can develop their brains with more energy. More energy makes a person more productive. So we need to avoid eating heavy food and eating heavily. Both of these drain a lot of energy. Our brain becomes unproductive without sufficient energy. So we should follow a balanced diet, our food should be easy to digest. We should always eat less than our hunger. If we have a hunger of eating 400 grams, then we should eat only 300 grams in combination with fruits. That is enough for us because it saves our energy, and that saved energy keeps the brain producing.

Learn To Increase Productivity

Learning can increase a person's productivity. A person should always try to learn new things. Learning can make your every task easy. A person who does not know how to do work correctly can never give productive results. So a person should learn work first, from someone or books. To be productive, a person should read productivity books as you are doing right now. There are many books available in the market that teach people to become productive and make the best use of time. A person who has learned work does it more efficiently and more accurately.

Find the top 10 books on your subject that you are interested in. Buy them all 1 to 10 and read them all. It will increase your skills and your skills will increase your productivity. By reading a book, you learn an author's lifetime experience in some pages, and you can implement it to change your life. "The more you learn, the more you earn" the more you learn about money, the more you earn the money. The more you learn about personality development, the more respect you get in society. The more you learn about useless stories and books, the more garbage goes into the brain. So read carefully. Choose books according to the required skills of your goal and read them to change your life.

Seek Knowledge From Other Sources

If you read about the 1900s society, you will realize that at that time, people had to look to other people for information. At that time, the only source of wisdom was wise people, who had some good information about the subjects. In this era, it is completely irrelevant because we have the internet and information available everywhere you don't have to go anywhere. You can find any information with just a single click. Now we don't need someone's experience to learn something new because we can find thousands of people's experiences on the internet. We don't need to go ask for small things from an experienced person. This is a smart generation, and we can learn by ourselves. We have thousands of sources of information.

One can learn from life-changing movies that inspire people, like biographies of billionaires. One may learn from online courses. Learning will never waste your time, it will return you in 1000 folds.

Type Of People And Productivity

Relaxed And Focused People

There are two types of people, first are those who work with a positive outlook and without pressure. They are productive and energetic in every situation. They can work consistently and be disciplined in every situation. They don't like pressure. These people do not get distracted easily. They can read books and do any work that needs to focus on a noisy environment. These people finish their tasks in advance. They do not get distracted by normal distractions like sex and food fragrances. They avoid pressure to complete their work. They complete their work without pressure. These are the focused and cool people.

Swami Vivekananda: once he was reading a book and a noisy wedding Barat with bands crossed from that place where he was reading a book. After some time some people asked him, did you see the Barat crossing from here, and he politely replied, no I was reading a book and I don't know about the Barat. It means he was so focused on reading, that he could not notice that a Barat crossed from there. Elon Musk is also one of those people whose focus is extreme in every situation.

People Who Work Better under Pressure

The second type of people is those people who feel less focused on normal situations. They get easily distracted in any distraction. They can't even read a book in a little noise. They don't take situations seriously until it's urgent. They work slowly until it's urgent and important. These are the people who finish their task on the last date. These people show incredible results in less time if they are under pressure. These people can convert work pressure into energy. These people focus better when they are under pressure. These people do not feel energetic until the last day of work submission. Distractions do not let them finish their work in relaxed situations. Where distractions don't distract them when they are under the pressure of work.

You may have noticed in your school that some students do not study for the entire year but before the 10 days of exam, they study a lot and perform awesome in exams. These guys can convert pressure into focus. These people need the pressure to focus. Without pressure or without understanding the urgency of the situation and work, they can not focus. Their distractions fly away when they are under pressure. It is nearly impossible to distract them when they are under pressure. They can even forget about their bad habits under pressure. These people require a deadline and pressure to do the work. They work better in the last days of the deadline. They are awesome in pressure. They are the best performers in bad situations. To develop high willpower, they require pressure and fear of losing.

People who fall in category number one, who work better in every situation should try all the techniques mentioned above.

People who work better on deadlines can also try all the techniques mentioned above. They should set deadlines for their every work and force themselves to do that work for a solid reason. Plus they should follow a special technique mentioned below.

Compulsion

People who work better under pressure, those people should always take big challenges to complete because only then, do they work better to achieve their goal. They can force themselves to do something. They can put any pressure on them to work more efficiently.

Time Management

As we have already discussed, everyone has the same 24 hours in a day. So it is not wrong to say that we have equal opportunity to use our time to achieve our goal. I have heard many people saying that they do not have time to do something good in their life. But when I ask about their schedule, they disappoint me, they all work for 6 to 7 hours a day. They have a schedule only for 6 to 7 hours in a day; they do not know where they spend the rest of the time. Many people say that they spend their leisure time on entertainment, whereas some housewives say that they do not have time because they have two children. So they can't do anything extra in their free time.

We all have 24 hours in a day. Achievers achieve their goals within these 24 hours. Because they know how to manage their time well. How to use the time to add value in life.

Once, my friend and I were talking about goals and success. She told me that she has two children and that is why she does not have time for herself. I asked about her goal and she replied that it is an administrative service, but she is not able to study for the administrative service exam because of the less time she has. So I told her a little story about a woman who had two children, and she was also doing a government full-time job, but she was not happy with her job because she wanted to become an IAS. She studied hard with her job simultaneously and cracked the IAS exam. Finally, she achieved her goal. After sharing this story, I asked my friend what your challenges are. How are you so busy, and you don't have time to achieve your goal? What do you do when your children take a siesta? She generously replied that she watches soap operas! We laughed about that. Then I told her that nobody discusses the story of a failed person. **Nobody asks about the struggle and difficulties that a loser faced in his journey. Nobody shows sympathy for a loser.** People only care about successful people. Nobody is going to ask about constraints that you faced to manage time. Nobody would care why you didn't have time to achieve your goal. Only success and achievements matter. Problems will always be there because this planet is full of problems. We can achieve our goals by defeating issues, excuses for problems do not help us to achieve anything. There will always be 24 hours in a day. There is no way to add more hours in a day. How can a person say that he will take action to achieve his goal when he will have time to do so. No one can create more time on this earth, so don't wait for free time. Give time to achieve your goal in every situation. There should be no delays in achieving your goal.

Everyone needs to set a schedule where they have to give time to achieve goals. So time management is really important to achieve goals. A busy person should block time to do something to achieve goals. We all have limited time, and we have to achieve success in a limited time. We will learn to deal with the distractions to save our time and save time to do something productive.

Social Media

You should never waste your time on social media in the early morning because it does not add any value in life, it fills garbage in the mind, and it can also ruin the entire day. If someone earns money from social media then it is completely fine to use it in the morning, but if not then it is a waste of time. Many people open social media in the morning just for a few minutes to see what is happening in the world of social media. But they fall into the trap as they open it, the brain starts releasing dopamine, and it feels happy to see more stuff on social media. It continues, and after some time people realize that it is already too late. So they run to get ready for work, and they lose the best time of the day on social media. It ends in the night when a person feels so tired after the day he realizes that he could do more, he could be productive, but he wasted the day. This is how people waste precious time daily. Time is precious and time management is all about doing important work to achieve your goal.

A productive person never wastes his morning time on social media. He always tries to do something productive in the morning time. Morning time is the most productive time for maximum people. So we should use this time to do something productive that can help to achieve our goal.

To avoid distractions, you can set silent notifications for social media. A person who gets easily distracted can even disable notifications. No one should spend more than 45 minutes a day on social media. Because 45 minutes a day are sufficient to spend on social media. Your social media circle should be progressive. There should be channels, pages, and people who motivate you to achieve your goal. Social media should add value to your life, and it should not waste your time. There are many accounts on Instagram and many channels on YouTube that can add value to your life. Use social media to benefit yourself. Use it to add value to your life.

News

News is important, but it is not urgent in the morning. If a person watches the news in the morning, it makes a person negative in the morning because it fills a person with negative emotions. Studies show that people who watch a lot of news see the world as less realistic as compared to other people. They find problems in every solution.

One of my known ones has a habit of watching the news whenever he has free time. He watches those useless debates that have no relevance in real life. As a result, he has many debates in his family, he is the only reason for not having happiness in the family. He ruins everyone's day with his negative words and mind that he subconsciously feeds in his mind from news channels.

I asked him what he would do after knowing all the debates. How it is going to help him. He replied it keeps me updated on the world. I asked him what do you do after that? Do you earn money from it? Is it making you successful, or is it helping you to get salvation? I was very much clear while asking him, I wanted to know the benefit of watching the news for a full day. Because I was also updated with every news that he knew by only watching 100 superfast news bulletins for 10 minutes. The actual news update is for ten minutes a day, and it should not take more than ten minutes. The rest of the time, people waste their time just to put garbage in their minds.

So obvious that a person has 100% garbage in his brain. He likes stupid people and hates wiser and rich people. He has a habit of talking bullshit with people. He treats his wife like an animal because he thinks that he knows everything and his wife is always wrong. He starts TV with the sunrise and watches it till midnight.

He has a lose-lose situation in his life, he is in double loss because of this habit. Once the wastes his precious time watching the news and second he is becoming the reason for the sadness and depression of his family. He stays in anxiety because of watching the news.

I understand that news is important for information purposes. But it should not cost you a lot of time. If someone wants to get updated with the news, then he can watch superfast 100 news in 10 minutes at the time of lunch on YouTube. This kind of news shows you can get more information in less time, and it can save time. News is only meant to give information. So watch it only for information purposes. Printed media is the best source of news because here you can read critical news according to need. It doesn't waste time creating suspense in the news. The main advantage is selective reading. It is not made for entertainment. It is made for information only, that is why Warren Buffett reads newspapers. He doesn't like to watch the news on TV. TV gives less news and wastes more time. TV shows have to maintain their TRP, and they also have to create stories to make it interesting for viewers, so they can earn money by showing advertisements. **"Watching the news in the morning is like taking a pill of depression in the early morning for the entire day"**. It is the worst beginning for the day a person can do.

Emails

Emails have no such effects, but they are distractive. When we can have a calm and focused environment, then why create distractions?

When talking about time management, everyone needs to create a special Email ID only for important updates like bank and stockbroker updates. It saves time because it does not have useless advertisements and emails to distract. This special email ID will have only emails that are worth your time. It will save your time when finding an essential email because here you only have important emails. Do not log in with this email ID on any social network, so they can't spam you.

So we need at least two email IDs to manage our time effectively. One email ID should be registered with all shopping websites, Social Media, YouTube, and for enrollment on online courses. Notifications should be disabled for this email ID. You can read your unimportant emails once a week on Sundays.

Registered the second one with the bank and brokers. This will save time because you have already categorized your emails into two categories: one for indispensable and urgent and another is unimportant and not urgent. So you can read all your critical emails daily, and it will not waste time.

This simple method will save you 2x time on emails, number one if you have any reference number, any verification number, any transaction details from Demat or bank, or any OTP then you will find it easily. You will not need to scroll thousands of unnecessary emails to find a critical email. The second mobile will not beep many times in a day.

Instant Messaging Apps

Instant Messaging apps have become an important part of our life. It helps us to be connected to essential people. But it can also be the biggest time-waster for those people who get easily distracted. It can waste a lot of time. So to manage time effectively, we need to limit the usage of instant messaging apps. Some people waste their time talking about useless things on instant messaging apps, whereas some waste their time discussing other people. As we have discussed before, discussing other people's lives is a waste of time, and it drains your energy on useless people. On the other hand, many people discuss their daily life and information related to the world by chatting. It has two bad sides when you chat with a person. First, we can not explain very well on instant messaging apps because we lack emotions. Second, it takes a lot of time to explain a small piece of information. The information takes hours to explain in chatting, which could be shared in a few minutes on a call. So avoid long conversations in chatting to save time. Call directly if you want to share some important information with someone. Drop a message only, if information can be shared in a single message. Think about where your information can be shared fast and choose that way.

You need to avoid unimportant and unnecessary conversations to save time. We all have those unimportant people who only send us Good Morning and Good Night messages, or sometimes they talk about other people and society. You need to avoid them to save time. To manage it, disable a less critical and disturbing person's notification. So they can not distract you.

Sleep Properly

After working hard for the day, people get tired. People feel unproductive after working for an entire day. So they choose to use their unproductive time to be spent on social media and instant messaging apps. People think that the nighttime is best for chatting and social media because they are not able to do something productive at night. It is somehow fine if these apps are used only for a maximum of 45 minutes, but it is a problem when a tired person spends 3 to 4 hours on social platforms. **By wasting a lot of time on social media, they waste their next day's productivity in advance.** Late-night sleep and late wake up in the morning and slothfulness because of late night. It also ruins the next day and this becomes the habit and people develop this kind of habit as result they become permanently unproductive people. (I recommend reading Robin Sharma's book 5 AM club to understand the importance of waking up early) To be productive, it is necessary to sleep properly for at least 7 hours.

Keynotes

- Doing more work with higher accuracy in the right direction in less time is called productivity.

- We all have time daily, when we are most productive, we can do more in that time.
- To increase productivity you can do meditation, yoga, and pranayam.
- Watching the news in the morning is like taking a pill of depression in the early morning for the entire day.
- **News gives you the tension of the universe, and that isn't worth your attention.**
- To manage time effectively, you need to manage your social media and email ID first.

XVII

Perfect Time To Defeat Procrastination

In this lesson, you are going to know some techniques to start working for your goal, defeating laziness and procrastination. You will know how to make your time perfect and how to use that time. You will know secrets to avoid procrastination and develop a doer's attitude. **The perfect time comes and you create it.** It came into my life because I created it, and it will also come into your life.

Sometimes it is impossible to do work in the right direction immediately. Sometimes we lack resources or a strong base. For instance: It is impossible to start a business without securing the family. Because you can take risks on yourself but should take risks on your family. So sometimes it is a need to wait for a while before taking a life-changing step.

We all are different, we can be inspired by anyone, but we implement the learnings in our way. I understand that humans feel tired, we feel broke sometimes. Everyone can't do great work in tension.

Sometimes you need to wait for a while before taking a step, you need to wait for opportunities. Till then, you must prepare yourself for that opportunity. A prepared person grabs better opportunities as compared to an unprepared person. **"We have to choose the perfect time and make situations favorable for that time because perfect time never comes, but you have to create perfect time"**

Perfect Time In Schools

We all had a habit of procrastination in our school days. When we used to say that "I will start studying from tomorrow" and the next day we used to repeat those golden words, "I will start studying from tomorrow". This is how we used to waste days. Then a day before the exam we used to start our study and feel that it would be great if we studied before. This was the reason for many students' bad scores in schools. To achieve our goals and become successful in life, we need to avoid procrastination.

Create Your Perfect Time

To avoid procrastination, choose a time when you think, you can make that time perfect. Set a perfect time, work to make it perfect. Ask yourself how that day will be perfect? What special will you have on that day? Is there any opportunity in the way which you are working for?

The time difference should be a maximum of 6 months from now. If you can't create any favorable situation in the next six months to achieve your goal, it means you can never create it. If today your situation is not favorable, then make it favorable in the next 6 months. So you can grab opportunities. For Instance: If you want to do a business, and you are postponing it because of a lack of knowledge and funds. Then learn the fundamentals and meet people who are already doing that business. Arrange enough funds to start a business. Prepare yourself mentally. Earn enough money for the family security. Keep money aside for the startup, do not spend startup money anywhere else, not in any situation.

Commit To Yourself

You have to be honest with yourself. Commit to achieving your goal. Commit to blocking time daily to achieve your goal. You have to work daily to achieve your goal. It doesn't matter what the situations are because time management and productivity are meaningless if you do not achieve your goal. You need to work consistently to kill procrastination. Forget about laziness, be hard on yourself, set daily deadlines to do something to achieve your goal. **Never commit anything that you don't mean to do, It creates a poor self-image. By committing fake commitments, your brain stops taking you seriously.**

Will Power

To work towards your commitment. You need to grow your willpower. Will power helps you to do work to achieve your goals in life. So I will tell you some techniques to grow your willpower. Techniques that can create a huge impact on your life. Techniques that will kill your procrastination habits and make you ready to do work.

Small Actions

To increase willpower, You have to work and feel successful. Small achievements are the best option to feel success. You can achieve small targets like losing 1 kg weight in a month. Clearing the online tests that increase IQ level, Daily running for 1 kilometer. These small actions will push you to achieve big goals. Because you have proven to your brain that achievements are easy, and it feels good to achieve. It increases willpower. After feeling achievement, your inner self motivates you to achieve more, and you will take more action.

Whenever you achieve something that you love, the brain releases dopamine. It makes you feel awesome. So take small actions and convert that action into small achievements. Daily achievements can develop an achiever's mindset. Finishing small tasks develops the feeling of achievement. Like: set a time to do meditation and yoga and finish it in that time, set daily rituals, and finish them successfully.

Take Challenges

In the second step, we go a little further to increase willpower. We start challenging ourselves, it is not necessary to take huge challenges, in the beginning, small challenges are enough to increase willpower like taking baths with cold water. This simple practice tells your brain that you are ready to do anything to achieve your goals. By taking a bath with cold water, the body, and brain both feel uncomfortable. It prepares the brain and body to be uncomfortable for the benefit if you do it daily. It sends a message to the brain that it is important to leave the comfort zone to achieve anything in life.

You can challenge people in small games where you can defeat them, it will also increase your willpower. You can take any challenge to increase your willpower. By taking challenges, your willpower will increase. By taking small challenges, you will get prepared for big challenges.

This life is full of challenges. We humans have to face challenges everywhere, every time in this life. Even I would like to say that human life is a challenge itself. It is a challenge to complete our mission of life, life is a **challenge to achieve the ultimate goal of salvation.** We prepare ourselves to face life challenges. This makes a person stronger.

Fulfill Promises

You may wonder what is the relation between fulfilling promises and willpower. But both of these have a direct relation. If you fulfill your every promise then, it sends a message to the mind that you are a person of your words. So the mind starts creating a personality, where you fulfill your every promise. As Lord Krishna says **"a good work brings more good work in your life, a bad work forces you to do more bad work"**. Your mind gets the motivation to develop a habit of fulfilling promises. When a person fulfills a promise, his willpower grows. Because fulfilling a promise creates a person's doer's personality. The person starts feeling good to fulfill promises, so he wants to fulfill more promises. A person feels trustworthy after fulfilling a promise, it feels good to be trustworthy and, Mind works to create your trustworthy image. To create a trustworthy image, it starts to develop high willpower because it has to fulfill promises. After developing a habit, the mind starts gaining the courage to fulfill commitments. You have to fulfill your promises outside your comfort zone. This is how you can be able to take appropriate action and kill procrastination. These are simple ways to avoid procrastination. You just have to start a good work or work in the direction of achieving your goal. **As Lord Krishna says "A good work brings more good work, a good habit brings more good habits, an achievement brings more achievements, a desire brings more desires**. So if you avoid procrastination, it will help to avoid more bad habits.

Perfect Time To Quit Bad Habits

You may have heard that quitting a bad habit is near to impossible. People take medicines to quit bad habits. People go to rehabilitation centers and pay thousands of dollars to quit their bad habits. This is Because of low willpower.

Many people say that they will quit their bad habits tomorrow. They procrastinate because they think that tomorrow will be the perfect day for them to quit bad habits like smoking and drinking, but their tomorrow never comes. Why don't they have the energy to quit a bad habit? Where does their motivation go after committing once? Motivation doesn't do miracles without willpower. These questions have only one answer, they don't have willpower. They never take challenges in their life. They prioritize their bad habits over their goal. **Lack of clarity in vision is the reason for having bad habits.**

To develop strong willpower we need a clear goal, vision, and a desire to achieve that goal. A clear goal is very important to develop willpower. This goal motivates and also gives willpower.

My friends ask me Rahul please, tell us the mantra, how did you quit smoking and drinking? I simply reply to them, I don't know any mantras. I decided that I will not smoke and drink. And I never touched those things again. Yes, it is that easy if you decide to quit those habits. Because I had a clear vision and goal for my future. I was ready to sacrifice my bad habits to achieve my goal. That is why I quit my bad habits. Whenever I visualized my future, I always felt that these bad habits should not be a part of my future. I realized that these bad habits are the biggest obstacles in the way of achieving my goal. I realized that these bad habits drain my energy, and it wastes my time. I believe that an addicted person can not do anything productive. Alcohol also damages neurons and cognitive functions of the brain, I found a lose-lose situation for consuming alcohol and smoking. I thought about brain damage and other damages caused by smoking. So for my productivity, time, and most important my goal, I decided to quit bad habits. My goal gave me the energy to quit it. My goal became the cause of my inspiration. Your goal can also become the cause of your inspiration. If you have a clear goal and enough dedication to achieve that goal. Keep your goal always in mind and then take actions accordingly and develop habits accordingly. I think no one could have the goal of becoming a smoking and alcohol addict. Dedicate yourself towards success, choose your goal, choose success and quit bad habits.

Side effects of Alcohol

There are many myths about the benefits of alcohol, but there is the only medicinal use of alcohol that can benefit. Consumption of alcohol as liquor only has side effects. There are many side effects of alcohol for the human body, but we will only discuss side effects related to the brain.

As a small molecule, alcohol can easily cross membrane barriers and reach different parts of the body very quickly. Attainment of its equilibrium concentration in different cellular compartments depends on the respective water content. Alcohol can affect several parts of the brain, but, in general, contracts brain tissues, destroys brain cells, as well as depresses the central nervous system. Excessive drinking over a prolonged time can cause serious problems with cognition and memory. Alcohol interacts with the brain receptors, interfering with the communication between nerve cells, and suppressing excitatory nerve pathway activity. Neurocognitive deficits, neuronal injury, and neurodegeneration are well documented in alcoholics, yet the underlying mechanisms remain elusive. The effect can be both direct and/ or indirect.

There are many side effects of alcohol, smoking, and other bad habits. These addictions can be the biggest obstacles in your life. You just have to clear your mind about what you want to do in your life. Quit all your bad habits whether it is a habit of procrastination, the habit of wasting time, the habit of watching porn, or the habit of using too much social media. Nobody should choose bad habits over goals. Intoxicants and other bad habits drain the willpower of a person, so it must be quit. A person must set goals in his life to quit bad habits and should have a clear vision to achieve that goal. **A person without goals in life is the same as a directionless boat that does not have to go anywhere, they only get lost in the sea.**

So, I have only one line summary of this paragraph for you, **"this is the perfect time to quit bad habits"**

Keynotes

- Create your perfect time.
- Prepare yourself to grab any opportunity.
- Commit to yourself and take commitments seriously.
- Increase your willpower to remove procrastination from your life.
- Take small actions, and fulfill promises to develop willpower.
- Quit bad habits now, this is the perfect time to quit every bad habit.

Want More?

We have discussed a lot of things in this book about becoming successful and achieving every goal. Now, what is left to achieve? It is money. It is a financial goal that everyone must have. Money is the main and most important need. It is a reality if you want to live a happy life, you need money for that. **Money can't buy happiness but money can buy things that you need to be happy.** Money has a direct relation to happiness. Everyone must understand and accept the fact that money brings happiness in life. Money brings mental peace in life. No one can be called an achiever in his life if he doesn't earn a good amount of money. You can't call yourself an achiever without money. In our era money is a synonym for success. You need money everywhere. A good person needs more money than a bad person because a good person can do more good with that money. So here in the end matter, we will know ways to manage money to achieve financial goals. We will know how to manage money and avoid debt.

Need Of Money And Money Management

Money is very important for humans. We can't deny the fact that a person cannot be called successful without money. Your achievements and accomplishments are measured by the money you have. Money and Success are synonyms in this era. At Least, this world determines success with money because money has an exchange value. We can buy services and goods with money. In the materialistic world, success is measured by a person's potential of buying goods and services. The more goods and services a person can buy, the more successful he is considered. So it is clear that to be successful we need money. Different people earn money from different sources. There are many ways to earn money. But **there is only one way to keep that money in your pocket and grow, that is good money management.**

It is really important to manage money to be rich. So in this lesson, we will know how to save and grow money effectively to become rich and successful.

Importance Of Money

We can't deny the importance of money. Money is critical to living a healthy life. But in some movies, so-called singers and poets have portrayed that money is the root of all evil powers. I heard many lines like these philosophers where they say "you were born with empty hands and will die with empty hands". People have made songs on these, but the main hypocrisy is they sing these useless songs to earn more money. Spoils people's minds to demotivate them. They try to show money as valueless in their songs, but they sing songs to earn money. They are just trying to fool you. Money matters a lot and a person should work to earn money. **You can't take money with you to heaven, but money can create heaven for you on earth.**

Love Needs Money

Movies and society have created an environment where money and love are enemies, where money and honesty are opposite words to them. People believe that love doesn't need money. Love is pure without money. Money spoils true love. But you see the hypocrisy of film writers and directors. First, they demean money in movies, they show that money is the obstacle to achieving love. They show it that money is nothing and only true love matters. They show poor people with big hearts and happy families, and rich people as bad people. They show that money is not important in life. But despite this, the purpose of the movies is to earn more and more money. This is their reality and hypocrisy.

The first thing to understand is that money makes it easy to marry your love. Money can remove barriers like religion, casteism, and racism. So it is not wrong to say that money allows you to marry your love. A rich man can marry his love. So always see money as an opportunity in your life. It is an opportunity to get married to your love.

I have read many social media posts that girls run after money. Girls leave their boyfriends because of their weak financial conditions. In many cases, a poor man's girlfriend marries a rich man and her boyfriend posts her photos and writes his dirty mind's shit below her photo. These kinds of boys never think that money is required for everything in life. I assume for a minute that a girl chooses a boy for the sake of her love but what next? Can a boy's pure love buy her food? We have needs and require money to meet the needs. Can pure love help a girl to meet her requirements? A girl's family is going to check the boy's income. If the boy does not have any income source, then how can he feed the girl? If you are a boy who has the same mindset that girls should not marry for money, ask yourself a question; **"will your future wife be able to buy a car in the exchange of love, or will the showroom accept payments in the form of love?"** Then what is the point of saying this entire shit that you choose to love, not money? Love can give you better sex that's it, without money it can not give you anything more. The lack of money in the family starts clashes between spouses when their needs do not meet. Love is incomplete without money. Lack of money is bad, not the abundance of money. Only losers say these lines like; a girl should run after their love. Many losers say that you can buy anything with money except love. How can guys say that a girl should run after love and leave her family disappointed When they are not able to earn money to prove their love? **Why do only girls need to prove love by sacrificing their dreams, why do not boys prove their love by earning a lot and making their girlfriend's dreams true?** Every girl has a family and her family will see the bank balance because they want to secure their girl's future, and I believe there is nothing wrong with this.

A Casanova who begs money from his father to buy clothes and accessories to show off. What can he give to his wife? Can he pay bills with his love and swag? Do banks have columns to pay in love or swag? Should a girl forget that she is a human, and she has some needs?

Only vile boys blame women for this reason. A gentleman knows how to earn money and keep his woman happy. Gaga boys hide their vileness with these kinds of stupid statements. They call girls greedy to hide their weakness because the reality is that they do not deserve a girl, they are not men because they can't prove their love. To satisfy their ego, they call their girlfriends greedy and gold diggers. Can anybody tell me **"Does it make sense to live with only love, without money?"** loser boys want a girl who should not think about her future and run after a poor boy who smokes a lot, but he loves her.

It doesn't make any sense, nobody can survive on love. Money is important to buy food. After marriage, a girl is not going to eat love. She has some needs. She has to think about her kids' future. It is not possible to give good education to children based on love. Schools do not ask how much you love your wife and family, school asks for money. If someone wants peace and love both, then money is critical. Because without money, love cannot give peace for a long time. As needs increase, humans need money to fulfill them. If someone does not have money then this unsatisfied desire creates dissatisfaction in relation, and it creates conflicts and conflicts steal the peace. This materialistic world requires money everywhere. **"Money will not take you to heaven but create a heaven on the earth". "Money will not go with you in the afterlife, rather it can give you everything in this life".** To live in this world, we require money.

"Goodness needs money"

If a person calls himself a good person, then he requires a lot of money to do good. If someone wants to feed poor people, it takes money. If someone wants to do good for the environment, then it requires money. If someone can plant 1000 trees per year, he can plant crores of trees per year with money and leverage people. If someone wants to donate, he also requires money. Money is required everywhere. **"Money is not everything, but it can do everything for you".** So we require money everywhere. It is impossible to transform more people's lives without money.

Unmanaged People And Money

If you give a 1 billion dollars cheque to a donkey, what will he do with that cheque? He is going to eat that cheque because he doesn't know the value of that cheque. He is going to eat it because he only knows how to eat. A Donkey does not know that he can buy everything with money in this world. Similarly, a person who does not know the value of the money does the same, he spends it all. How can he become rich?

Unmanaged people do the same as donkeys do. Every Time they get paid, they go and buy new clothes. They go to expensive restaurants for dinner to show their friends that they have money to spend. They buy expensive clothes and watches to show that they are rich. To maintain their fancy lifestyle, they spend their whole salary within the 10 days of the month. This cycle repeats itself every month. When they get a bonus, they buy luxury items, drink premium whiskey and say yeah man you deserve it, because you have earned a lot of money. Their expenses increase in a ratio to their income. They believe that it is necessary to increase the expenses in the income ratio. That is why they remain poor for their lifetime. They do the same as donkeys do. They also eat the money as the donkey ate, but they eat it differently they eat it by unnecessary spending. **People don't remain poor because of lack of money, but because of lack of money management.**

KBC Winner

In 2011, A person won Rs 5 crore in KBC. He was from Bihar (his name will be secret due to privacy reasons) after which he gained fame. In a Facebook post, He revealed how the worst phase of his life started after winning KBC.

He wrote, "2015-2016 was the most challenging time of his life. He didn't know what to do. He became a local celebrity and would attend many programs in Bihar. As he was a local celebrity, he took the media very seriously in those days. He felt ashamed to say that he doesn't do anything. So for the sake of media interviews, he started many businesses so he would tell them about the business. However, those businesses would collapse after a few days."

A Lot Of People Cheated Him

He said that he got actively involved in charity, but later realized it was all a farce. He claimed that he attended many charity programs after KBC and he did charity many times, but people cheated on him. Because of his money, he was in the eyes of thugs, everyone was trying to grab money from him.

He Moved To Mumbai

As an average person who has big dreams thinks that movies are the best options to earn money, he also moved to Mumbai to become a filmmaker. He stayed in Mumbai for six months, and during this, he would smoke a full packet of cigarettes in a day. He became an alcoholic. After winning KBC, he started considering him as an unlucky person because his life was fully disturbed. After winning KBC he became an addicted person who doesn't know what to do exactly, he wasted his money.

He Is Happy Without Money

After six months spent in Mumbai, He came back home and started selling milk again he spent all his money and became poor again.

He lost his mental peace because of mismanaged money. After some time he lost all of his money due to bad management of money. He was trying to show people that he is a businessman, but he did it without knowledge. He said that he also tried philanthropy, but people cheated on him.

He just blamed people and money for destroying his mental peace. He blamed money for every bad thing happening in his life. He portrayed money as a villain. He blamed the media for his business losses because of their interview he started a business. He blamed people for not being fair with him because people cheated on him, because of money. He blamed money for his bad habits, alcohol, and smoking. Money became his worst dream. It is the same as a donkey saying that everybody uses him for their benefit. This was not people's mistake if they used him because people have to benefit themselves, it's your duty to protect yourself. This is what a mismanaged person does. These are the consequences of mismanagement.

Here we can see that this person had the knowledge to earn money, but in the end, that money became his enemy because of a lack of money management knowledge. It is true, money is the enemy of mismanaged people.

This is why 99% of the people of the world have 57% of the total money of the world and the remaining 1% of people have 43% of the total world's money.

The amount of money doesn't matter for a mismanaged person, a person who can not manage $1 lac, how can he expect to manage $10 million. **It is the same as a person expecting to lift 100 kg, who can not even lift 10 kg. People do the same when it comes to money.** They say that I have only $1000, that is why I am not managing it. I will manage it if I have $1000000. He only blames the system and is good for not giving him $1000000. He doesn't prove his ability by managing $1000. **"If a person can manage one dollar, then he can also manage the 1 billion dollars".**

My Neighbor

My neighbor got a check of INR 38 lacs in 1970 from the government because his land was acquired by the government for road construction. It was a huge amount at that time, if we compare it with gold value then it would be 766304347 today. He was a Casanova. He didn't save money. Even though he didn't buy a house. He spent his life in a hut. Now that person has zero in his account, he is fully dependent on his son for his health treatment. He is an asthma patient.

So here it could be understood that lack of money is not the problem, lack of knowledge about money management is the real problem. Money reflects the true self of a person. If a good person has money, he spreads goddess to society, if a bad person has money, he spreads more badness to society. If a stupid person has more money, he does more stupid stuff with that money. If an idiot has money, then he does more idiotic stuff.

A Businessman

A billionaire businessman had two sons. He left a Billion of dollars business empire for them. His wife divided his empire between his sons equally. Both were ambitious, both were well-educated from the best universities. Both invented many new systems in Indian financial systems. Everything was well in their life for the next fifteen years. Both had equal wealth. The younger one had digital and technologically advanced businesses. So he had an advantage over his brother. But his many businesses started disrupting because he had huge debts. His many companies went bankrupt. But somehow he was successfully managing his one digital and technology-friendly company. He did well with it for the next few years but after the entry of a new player in the market. His business got disrupted badly. New players destroyed the competition in the market and many companies went out of business. After four years, he filed for bankruptcy.

This is the story of a billionaire who failed to keep his inherited wealth. I have many such examples where the heirs of the billionaires failed to remain wealthy. Why does it happen? Because people don't know how to manage money. How to sustain wealth. 90% of people have very good skills of making money, but they don't know how to keep it or how to grow it. People are not even able to manage money which they got in inheritance. Many people have been fortunate to have a lot of money in their life, but have nothing in their bank account.

Needs or Desires?

People do the same thing as a donkey does with the money they eat. If a person earns one million dollars in a month and spends it all by the end of the month, then what is the difference between a donkey and a man? Many people are in worse condition than a donkey because they earn later and spend first. People who buy cars on finance do the same; they have advance plans to kick out the money from their bank. They have plans in advance to spend money. They behave like their banks are not able to handle money. They don't say hi to money, they just kick out money from their door. It seems that they have animosity with the money.

Studies prove that the middle class increases their expenses in the same ratio of increasing income. This is the main reason they never grow rich in their life because they dig graves for their income in advance.

People with a mediocre mindset increase the size of their car as their income increases, but they never grow the size of their investment. **The Middle Class doesn't increase investments because they can't show off about growing investments, they can't impress society with their investments.** They buy expensive cell phones, and they increase the size of their house. I am not against increasing the size of cars and other luxuries. I am only a supporter of increasing my net worth and becoming wealthy.

THE REAL PROBLEM

Many people want financial freedom. They want a lot of money, but they never set any financial goals for themselves. It is the same as aiming, without any specific TARGET. The Aim should be clear. As I mentioned before, a person should be clear 100% on his goals. And the second is money management, it is really important. Because money does not like a person who doesn't know how to manage it. To meet financial goals, money management is a necessity. **Financial planning without the planning of spending is the best financial plan.**

Keynotes

- Money is so critical in life, you can't take money with you to heaven, but money can create a heaven for you on earth.
- You must prove your love by earning a lot of money.
- **Being rich and wealthy is the only trend that never goes out of fashion.**
- **To prove your abilities, you must start by earning money.**
- An unmanaged person can never have money.

- People who do not know how to manage money can never be wealthy.

Money Management

THE SOLUTION

There is a need to manage money effectively to become rich. The only solution for a mismanaged person is effective money management. It doesn't matter what your goal is, money management needs to be there to achieve any financial goal.

Effective money management

Money comes and goes, but to keep money in your pocket you need to manage it effectively. Because a well-managed small amount of money can make a person wealthy, and a person remains poor even after having trillions of dollars if managed wrongly.

We have seen people in our society who earn a lot but still cry for money. We all have those people who earn for their whole life, but they always remain in debt. All middle-class people have different sources of income, but at the end of the month, there is nothing left in their bank account.

Many times, when I tell people that they should invest in the stock market, they simply reply that they don't have enough money to invest in the stock market. Many of them say that they are already in debt. **Many people say that they have less income compared to their expenses. They never explain, that if they have less income, then how do they bear these extra expenses?**

THE TRADITIONAL WAY

There is a famous and successful money management system. It worked for millions of people, and it has made millions of people wealthy. This way is excellent, and most of the self-made millionaires follow it. In the traditional way of becoming wealthy.

Here we focus on Six main pillars.

- Security(Child education, health, family protection)
- Investment for Passive and leveraged Income
- Investment in Education
- Donation
- Expenses on needs
- Long term needs(Home, Car,

Security

In the corona crises, everyone realized the importance of security. Everyone realized that life can be temporary, jobs can be temporary and anyone can be fired at any time because of crises. Many people have learned this lesson after paying a huge cost. But everyone has realized that security is important, and money management can help in this. We must have enough money to survive for a year without doing anything, this is called security. It should be for a minimum period of one year. Your bank account should have money to survive your family for at least one year without doing anything. It can be 1 lac or more according to the living standards and area where you live. If you live in a rural area then less money could be enough and if you live in a large city then one lac may not be enough for you. You should calculate your monthly expenses, multiply them by 12 and save that much money in your bank account. This money will give you mental peace, this money will give you the courage to take risks.

For sickness and accidents, a person should always have life insurance and health insurance. It should be the priority, to secure his family from all unfortunate unexpected circumstances. If a person has covered his life and health with insurance and has enough funds to pay his children's fees, he can get rid of tensions and work peacefully. So a person should save 10% of his net income to secure his family.

Investment

For investment, a person must save 10 percent of his net income and invest it in various assets. The famous book The Richest Man In Babylon has mentioned this method in brief. That book mentions that a person who wants to be wealthy should save at least 10% of his gross income. It doesn't matter that the person is under debt or debt-free, he has to save 10% in every situation. Further 10% should be invested wisely. If a person does not know how to invest in a rewarding asset, then he can take expert help. Money should be invested with expert people. A person can also invest this 10% in his own business. Profits and returns earned on this investment should be reinvested.

Education Fund

Traditional money management methods say that one should always keep learning and should always keep a special fund aside for learning. At Least 1 percent should be invested in education. As Warren Buffett says, **"The best investment I have ever done is the Investment in my learning"**. Warren Buffett is right. Education is the most important factor in life. Learning deserves a special budget. Because **"investment in learning pays the best returns"**, again this was Warren Buffett's quote.

What happens when you invest in learning? You learn new skills and you earn more. Learning helps you in every way, learning is like sharpening the saw. When a person cuts many trees, he needs a break to sharpen his saw, because after sharpening the saw a person can cut more trees. Learning is the same when our skills get older, then we require new skills to earn more. We can earn a limited amount of money, with knowledge. In this era, our learnings become common in 18 months. It means if a person has read a book in a month, then this information is going to be common in the next eighteen months. So we need to learn new skills every day, every time. If we want to be successful in our life, if we want to be wealthy in our life, then we need to learn every day because the next generation is smart. So we need to allocate between one and ten percent of our money to learn new skills. So we can run faster than the rat race. We must be smarter than the next generation to be irreplaceable.

Donation

The Great Ancient Vedas say that if you give to the poor then this universe gives you in multiples. It is an automated system that works every time. So if you want more, then you have to give more. You may have seen that maximum rich people are philanthropists. Bill Gates and Warren Buffett are the best examples of this. This factor is common in every successful person's life. They love to donate, they love to help other people, they love to do philanthropy. So it is important to return to this universe what we have earned because this is the universal law.

To get something new and more, we need to return everything that we take from the universe. For instance, we return carbon dioxide to breathe-in oxygen. This is the universal law. This **universe always gives us more and better than what we return to it. We give it carbon dioxide, and in return, it gives us oxygen.** This process is more of receiving than giving. The universe always gives us multiple and more valuable things. It works similarly with money. If we return a penny to the universe, then it gives us in dollars. If we return in dollars, then it gives us back in thousands of dollars. So returning wealth to the universe by donating is also a way of increasing wealth. I am not talking about donating entire wealth, but at least you should return one percent to this universe for giving us such an abundance and opportunities.

Governments charge income tax on a concept where it is believed that the tax payee has earned money by using resources and opportunities of the nation. That is why governments charge taxes on the name of a nation and resources. **Donating money is**

the same as giving back to society for using the resources and opportunities of society. It is gratitude for giving you what you have. So you should start returning in small amounts, then this universe will give you more to distribute. Start donating without any personal interest, just donate to return to the universe.

Money donated to political parties to be on their good list is not called a donation, this is a business because it has some personal interest. Donation for exemptions in tax; is also not a donation. When you give the remaining money after expenses, then it is called begging. **Donation is when you give before your expenses.** You should have a routine to donate every month. A person can donate 1-10% of his income, according to his comfort. I have seen the magic of donating, my life transformed when I started donating money. You can also try it to transform lives and get more.

Needs And Other Expenses

This part of expenses can be the reason for failure in every part of money management and most of the people are not rich because they spend most of their income only here. People earn money and spend it all for their needs and desires. We need to manage this. This includes our daily needs, food, mobile, travel, and parties. So we have to limit it and adjust to achieve our financial goal, so we should not spend more than 40-60% of our income on this.

Long Term Needs

People get confused here. They think that these needs or desires are their goals, and they blunder. Now, what are the long-term needs or desires? These are the desires that confuse people, and it steals most of the chances of becoming rich. Because people think that buying a car is his goal and he should have a car, and he spends all of his savings on that car. But this is the wrong way to use money. People think that these desires are important for them. And the second mistake they make is spending all their savings on this. They think the car is their asset, but it becomes their liability because they will have to work for the car to repay the car loan's installments. If your asset is not giving you money it means you don't have an asset, you have a liability. An asset works for you and gives you money. This is the simplest definition of an asset.

So according to the traditional method of money management a person should open a different bank account for this purpose, and he should save at least 10% of his income for buying a car, a home, or anything else that he considers as his long term need or desire. This amount can be invested in safe investments like government bonds index funds etc. until it grows to buy a car or house.

Conservative Method of Money Management

I have discussed all the traditional ways to save money and create wealth now. If you are still not satisfied, then congrats, I have an advanced money management system for you. This method is only for those people who want to be rich but are facing difficulties in saving money. This method is only related to savings and investment; other methods will remain the same. This method has personally benefited me a lot. I have seen the magic of this method. I have personally created it for myself and now after seeing its success I am sharing it with everyone. I have tried it on many people, and they also have enjoyed the same magic of this method, and the most beautiful thing about this method is that you save money to become rich without even realizing it. It does not impact your spending habits. So let's discuss it, every time you buy anything you have to fix a deal with yourself that you will buy a thing for 10% less money. For example, if your budget for buying shoes is 100 dollars, then buy shoes only for 90 dollars and save 10 dollars in your conservative bank account. Either take a 10% discount or buy a pair of shoes priced at 90 dollars only. In every situation, you have to spend less than your budget and save the rest of the 10% for creating wealth. Every time you buy anything, you have to save 10 percent for wealth creation. Invest that 10% amount in good and high return assets and forget about that money for the time until it becomes a huge amount of money.

You have to assume that you have already spent that money. It will psychologically make you feel like you have already spent that money. You will not have a mental burden or pressure for that money, because that money was meant to be spent by you. So you can relax about the risk of losing that money in investment. With this mindset never think about that money, even not in tough times.

10% is the minimum percentage for the essential item purchases. While talking about luxury items, **savings also must be luxury with them. You must keep 50% of your money aside from luxury purchases. For example, if you were about to buy shoes for $1000 then save $500 for your wealth creation account and spend $500 to buy shoes**. If you believe that your item will not remain a luxury if you save half of the budget money. For example, if you were about to buy a pair of shoes worth $1000 and after saving 50%, you feel that shoes worth $500 are not luxury in your eyes. Then double your budget. Set a budget of $2000 to buy the shoes and buy shoes for $1000 and save $1000. By doing this you will save double money, and you will also have luxury items. Similarly, you can save whenever you buy unnecessary and luxurious things, like expensive perfumes, parties, smoking, expensive hotels, expensive food, etc. (but if you spend on alcohol or any other bad habit then you should save 200% of your expense because it will also help you to treat side effects). Here you have an opportunity where your luxury expenses can contribute to creating luxurious wealth.

Just try this method for one year, and it will transform your life forever. This is the method I used to implement in my life when I started saving because I faced difficulties in saving. This method will also impact your life.

Keynotes

- Money management is the root to become wealthy.

- Family security comes at first.
- You need to invest money to become rich.
- Investments in education pay the best returns.
- When you donate money, it comes in a thousand folds back to you.
- Don't spend money to show off and to fulfill unnecessary desires.
- Save money for your long-term needs, if you save money now, then money will save you in your tough times.
- Always save at least 10% of your expenses, to become wealthy.

Debt Management

In the modern age, people have two major money problems, one excess debt and the second excess lending money to someone and he is not returning. These two are the major issues that everyone is facing. Both of these should be managed effectively to accomplish your financial goal and be successful in money management.

Debt

There are two types of debt, 'good debt' and bad debt. Good debts are those debts that put money in your bank, and bad debts are those debts that put out money from your bank. This is the simplest definition of debt. These days one concept is getting very popular called easy EMI. This scheme is a trap. This concept is a win-win situation for both, Government and finance companies. They are all running good businesses. Consumers are falling into the trap of desire. Consumers only pay a down payment of 10% of the full cost of goods. Companies finance 90% of the amount. In some cases, companies finance 100% of the goods without any down payment. This concept is booming the demand in the white goods sector and the finance companies' shares are trading at the PE of 140 to 150. Because investors know that these companies will earn more profits. Investors know about the rat race and the buyer's irrational behavior.

On the other hand, consumers are becoming poorer and spending their earnings in advance. Consumers are spending in advance. Because they have become the slaves of their desires. Why did I call them slaves? Because they buy things in advance on EMIs and work on that later. This is a slavery mindset, a slave works for his master. Here, desires became these people's master. The same people are working for their desires. For example, a person buys a mobile phone on EMIs. He would pay EMIs for three to four months in enthusiasm. After that, he realizes that he is no longer interested in that mobile phone, but he still has to pay the EMIs because it is his obligation now. He is a slave where he doesn't want a thing, but he still has to work to repay EMIs. He works like a slave, slaves work without interest, enthusiasm because they are helpless. **A person also becomes a helpless slave by buying on finance.**

Many people only consider the monthly installment and think that this is a small amount. They don't think that they are becoming slaves of unnecessary desire. They think that a small amount of money doesn't matter, but they never realize that if they had saved this money, then this money can create huge wealth for them. (For example, minimum $50 (₹3750) SIP per month for the 15 years would be $45960.44 (₹3447033) at the return rate of 18 percent per annum)(exchange values as of 1-1-2022). So it was not only $50, it was 1000 times more than that. Always spend after calculating the future value of the money.

Companies know the fact that they can manipulate people by showing advertisements, where they use words like easy EMI and small installments. They know that people are not going to consider the power of compounding, they know that nobody is going to calculate the long-term loss of unnecessary expenses. Companies advertise it as convenience and market it as something that helps a person to fulfill desires. Even though he does not need the new gadget, but still buying it because he thinks that he is spending only $50 now and $50 is not a big amount for his convenience. He thinks that $50 cannot impact his pocket, and it doesn't matter to spend $50.

A person may think that these EMIs are too small. What if a person will enjoy new gadgets or fashion in EMI because it has small installments. So it is not about the EMIs, it is about the habit that he is building. Isn't it stealing the future fortune, earnings, and prosperity today? Don't you think that you have an opportunity to make $45960.44 by just saving $50 per month? On the other hand, if you spend $50 just to be trendy and look dashing. However, this trend is also going to be out of fashion, and you are still going to be out of trend and poor. **In this case, you are going to be out of**

fashion plus poor. If you buy an expensive watch on EMI, then you are more likely to buy more things on EMIs. As we discussed desires vs goals. After some years you will only have old mobile phones and outdated TV and old washing machines plus debt. **On the other hand, if you spend only on needs and save only $50, you will have $45960.44 in 15 years by just controlling your unnecessary expenses.** (And this is not the maximum amount that you can have because once you build a habit of saving and investing then you will invest more and earn more), **money is 90% about habit and 10% about earning.**

EMI's are similar to kicking out money from the door. Isn't it bad to spend before earning? If a person spends money before earning, then the savings can never exist in the person's life. He will forever lack the money. This is about building a habit, a person who builds a good habit of saving and investing, he never lacks money. He invents ways of investing money in a good place. On the other hand, if a person develops a habit of unnecessary spending, he only invents new ways of burning money. **You don't become rich by looking rich, you become rich by rich habits.**

Finance companies and commercial advertisements show it as royal and classy because that is part of their business. They do not have any headaches for the sake of consumers' financial goals. They are tigers, and consumers' pockets are goats for them.

First, this concept will never let you save money, second, it drags you into the debt trap, third, it forces a person to spend on unnecessary expenses. It changes consumers' mentality.

EMIs are bad debt, it puts out money from the bank. Everyone should avoid this type of debt. These are the pitcher leaks, these holes never let you achieve your financial goal. Every leakage of money should be stopped, this is the only way of achieving financial goals.

Debt For a Car

Two friends, Ridhima and Maan completed MBA from the same university. Both are placed in the same company. Maan started living in his rented flat to maintain his lifestyle. He has some friends whom he has to throw parties with every Saturday night. He purchased a new car worth INR 10 lac (13,401.59USD (exchange values as of 1-1-2022)), INR 1 lac (1,340.16USD) was a down payment and 9 lac (12,059.37USD) was financed. His salary was good, he never faced any difficulty in paying installments. Everything was great in his life. He was an intelligent and talented person, after one year he got a promotion. After six months, he got another promotion because of his skills. To show his upgraded lifestyle, he purchased another luxury car. Again, this car was 80% financed. At the age of 28 he got married, he got busy in life.

On the other hand, Ridhima had the same need for a car as Maan had, but due to her weak financial background, she had to support her family. So she managed a year traveling by cab. After one year, she saved enough to purchase a new car. But she decided to save money to support her family. So she purchased a second-hand car. After 2 years, Ridhima got her first promotion. She had a clear vision of becoming rich. After 5 years, she saved 30 lacs INR (40,203.15). So she decided to start a business. She started the business. After some time she got married at the age of 30 years and at that time her net worth was 3 crore rupees(3,99,597.60 United States Dollars (on 1-1-2022)).

On the other hand, Maan was still paying the installment of his new car. He was busy maintaining his lavish lifestyle. He had nothing in his bank account, and he had liabilities to pay.

In this story, we can see how a person can build a fortune by investing money at the right time. A person's financial goal should be creating huge wealth. Priority should be earning millions, not showing off, and expenses to maintain a fake lifestyle.

Spending an unnecessary $1 is not spending of only that one dollar, it is the loss of all opportunities that one dollar could bring to you. It is the loss of thousands of dollars in the future. Whenever I spend $1, I always see it as the future's thousands of dollars. I always ask this question: what could be the future value of this dollar and what could be the best use of this dollar.

If you need to buy a car, then you should never buy it on heavy finance and heavy interest. Rather than, you should save money to buy a car and grow that money by investing. You should save the amount every month, which would be installments of a car, and open a separate Demat account to invest that money in top-performing index stock.

There is a famous philosophy used by finance companies: buy today, pay tomorrow. I am against this philosophy. My philosophy is: **"save today, invest tomorrow and buy ovrmorrow".**

For instance, If a person buys a car worth 10 lac rupees(13,329.96 USD(as 1-1-)) on finance at the rate of interest of 12.2 percent per annum then he will pay ?735554(9,804.91USD) as interest in ten years. It means a car worth 10 lac rupees cost him a total of ?1735554 (23,134.87 United States Dollars) Which is not a good deal at all.

On the other hand, if he doesn't have the urgency of buying a car, and he saves the EMI of ?14463 (192.79) per month and invest that in the index fund that gives at least 15% minimum return then his money will be ?4030220 (53,722.67 United States Dollar) in ten years. After ten years he can buy a car worth ?10 lac, and he will have savings worth ?3030220(40,392.71 United States Dollars). It sounds good, but sometimes people have the urgency of buying a car, then a person can buy a second-hand car and still can save money for the next ten years.

On one side you will spend ?1735554(23,134.87 United States Dollars(1-1-2022)) and on the other side, you will save ?3030220(40,392.71 United States Dollar). It is not just about buying a car, it is all about making a smart decision. Smart decisions lead to more smart decisions and save you from debt.

This is how financially successful people think. They don't fall into the debt trap. **Healthy investing habits make you wealthy.** Money is fuel, nothing is possible without money. One healthy financial decision leads to another healthy financial decision. So according to me, a car loan is a bad loan. To become a millionaire, you have to do nothing extraordinary, just avoid such 4-5 loans.

Credit Card

Using a credit card is the same as taking your boss for an advance. Credit cards can become a disaster to a person who has no control over his desires. Credit cards charge a 40% interest rate on late bills. Credit card companies want you to default the bill payments because they earn money when you default. It's their business. People who do not have control over themselves should avoid credit cards. A good financial planner never prefers the use of a credit card. Credit cards can become the worst nightmare for a person who can't control his expenses. It can be beneficial to those people who have better control over their desires, let's discuss.

Credit cards give interest-free credit for 40–50 days. If a person has $5000 in his bank account for expenses, then the person can use $5000 from the credit card, and he can earn interest on savings of $5000. He can also use those $5000, to grab short-term opportunities. It is not about becoming a miser. Rich people never let any leakage flow out of their money, that is how they become rich. You should save wherever you can save money to become wealthy. Credit cards should be used as debit cards. A person should only spend an amount that he already has in a bank account.

I will say it again: this is not about the small amount or large amount, it is about the habit, it is about developing a rich mindset. To become rich you should develop a rich mindset, you have to think like a rich person. Do not ignore your mind's ideas to invent money. If you ignore the idea of inventing a small amount of money, then the mind never generates Ideas to invent a large amount of money. By ignoring, you sent a message to the mind that the idea of earning a small amount of money was useless. Don't generate these kinds of ideas again. My mind says, "ok! I won't go in that direction. Minds do not work without appreciation. It assumes that generating ideas or inventing money was a waste of energy. For Instance: if you give a burger to a friend, and he replies that you're stupid, why don't you feed me with cheese and pizza. If he says," Why didn't you give him mutton, chicken, and liquor? What would you do with that guy? possibly you will be disappointed and never feed him again. Similarly, the mind does not show us better ideas of inventing money if we don't encourage it in its small ideas.

Let's come back to the topic: The second benefit of the credit card is the Credit score. If someone uses a credit card wisely, then he can use it to improve his credit score. Credit cards are the best way to create a good credit score. If someone uses this simple and easy approach of using a credit card, then he can create a good credit score. So in the future, he can have better opportunities to get a loan to start a business. But if a credit card is used to satisfy desires, then this could be the worst loan. For people who have a lot of desires, I would like to say it again, it develops a habit of spending before earning. This habit can be the biggest obstacle in the way of creating wealth.

Personal loans

This is another type of bad debt because maximum people take personal loans for their desires. These are the debts that have a very wrong impact on life. These loans are designed to force a man to increase their unnecessary desires. Human nature is very clear about expenses and luxury, humans spend more if they have easy access to debt. You may have heard that rich people's children do not value money, but why so? Because they have easy access to required cash, (but this is not the case with every rich person. Ultra Rich people always teach the value of money to their children). If a person does not have access to easy cash then he works hard to get those things, he uses his brain to invent money. If human needs are easily satisfied by loans, then he never generates thoughts of inventing money. He only generates thoughts of repaying debt. Working for the repayment of debt is the worst situation. We all have heard about financial freedom, but what is financial freedom? To understand it, we need to understand freedom. Working for yourself without any pressure and doing what is right for you is called freedom. A person who is derived by his unnecessary desires is the slave of his desires. **A slave is an unhappy person who works under another person or system in compulsion, where he feels helpless but can't escape**. Humans become slaves of debt by choice. They choose slavery over freedom.

Personal loans are for those who are slaves of their desires. A person becomes a slave two times when he takes a personal loan to fulfill his desire, first he becomes a slave of his desires when he does everything to fulfill his desires. Then, second, he becomes a slave of loan. He has to work to repay the loan. He has accepted a loan as his master's. It doesn't matter if he wants to repay the loan or not. His happiness doesn't matter now, he just has to pay the loan in every situation. It is a compulsion for him.

For instance; you took a personal loan for appliances purchase and luxury home decoration. But after some time you fade up from the decoration, so what is next? You still have to repay the loan. In this situation, first, your desire made you a slave, then desire handed over you to the loan.

So this is all about the personal loan. So everyone should avoid personal loans. For those people who take personal loans for health-related issues and family-related issues, I have already mentioned in the money management lesson about a special budget for health and emergencies.

So in conclusion, I would like to say that nobody should take personal loans. People should have good financial planning. People should learn to delay their unnecessary desires. It happens many times when we feel the urge to buy a new device and when we don't buy it and keep it on the waiting list, then after some time our urge and excitement of that thing automatically vanishes.

Home Loan

A bank-financed home can never be an asset. Despite this, I do not support those philosophies where people say that one should not buy a home because a home is not an asset. Rather, I believe that in bad times a home is the best support for a person. A person who does not have a home can be thrown out any time from his rented house. So buying a home is necessary, but a person can buy a home smartly. A person should first set another stream of income to pay home loan installments. A person can join a part-time business or generate passive income to pay installments of the home loan. Because owning a home is important, I always defend the idea of buying a home. But I never defend the Idea of wasting money on buying a home. Because investment should be at the right place, not on emotions. Buying an expensive house is a bad decision for those people who spend more than needed on buying a house. People spend their maximum savings on buying a house. And in maximum cases, they spend their savings and also take out a loan to buy a dream house.

Home is essential security for a family and one should not take risks with his family. But markets and large cities are designed to do business and jobs, that is why land prices in cities are high. Large cities are the worst option to buy a house. Only fools and ultrarich people should buy houses in the large cities. Because **fools do not have any financial goal and the ultrarich people don't care about finance.** So a person who wants to buy a house for family security should buy a house in a rural area. The properties in the countryside are 70-80% cheaper than in the city. In this situation, he can have money and security, so it is a win-win situation. Buying a house in the market area can become the biggest liability because properties are always overvalued in cities. The reason behind the overvalued properties is the valuation based on the business point of view. **So having a home is a necessity, but it is not necessary to have a home in the market area or large cities until the buyer is ultrarich or foolish.**

Business Loan

It is difficult to build a business without a loan but not impossible, so try to build a business without taking any loan. But sometimes starting a business with the help of a loan is easy and time-saving, so a person may consider a loan to build a business. Business loans can put money in your pocket. These loans can be considered good loans if they give you a handsome return. These loans can help a person to grow his wealth. These loans can be called appropriate risk in life, other loans are just compulsions or foolishness. But business loans have a direct relation with wealth creation. Even big, giant businesses take loans to grow their business. This loan can give a wealth boost if managed effectively.

Business loans bring many opportunities, but it doesn't mean that it can't be a bad decision for a person. It should be used smartly. A person who takes an excess business loan can drag him into the debt trap. So here I have some golden principles for a person who wants to start or grow a business with the help of a loan. A person who is starting up a new business should use 50% of his limit of the loan, and he should save the remaining 50% for better opportunities or repayment in difficult situations.

An established business should not use more than 40% of its asset value. Because expansion should be calculated and trials must be at a small scale first. Taking an excess risk can destroy a business, you may have heard that becoming rich is not difficult, but remaining rich is. Many businesses get success in their starting and after a few years, they take excess debt in the enthusiasm and fail. So a person should always take a balanced approach. Money needs management everywhere, that is why every bank has a manager to manage the bank. In every house, there should be a money manager. Every business should have a money manager.

Lending

Once there were two friends. Their names were Arun and Nayan. After passing secondary school, Nayan went to Mumbai to pursue mechanical engineering. Their bonding was good. They used to talk daily on the phone. Once, Arun went to Mumbai to meet Nayan. Arun phoned Nayan and asked him to come to meet him. After a long wait, Nayan arrived and met Arun, they started roaming in Mumbai streets. Nayan told Arun about his college and friends, and Arun discussed his life with Nayan. They spent the day together. When Arun was coming back home, Nayan asked for money and told Arun that his debit card expired, and he had to pay the room rent. Arun gave him money to pay rent. After some days, Arun's bike was damaged badly in an accident, so Arun asked Nayan about his debit card. He told Arun that his debit card is working now. Then Arun told him about the accident. Arun asked Nayan to return the money to repair his bike. Nayan immediately cut the phone and blocked Arun on every social platform. The amount of money was not much there, but the lesson was big.

I know many people may think that these types of blunders are normal in life, but these types of blunders are those tiny holes of the bucket that can empty the bucket. As I will go ahead, it will be clear that the effects of these types of blunders can be large. **"The Amount of money one has can create a difference in the size of the mistake, but it can not guarantee to avoid making a mistake"** The mistake Arun made with the small amount, many people do with their life savings.

A Businessman

I know a businessman who had an awesome business. He had huge profits in the beginning years of his life. As time passed some of his buyers defaulted as a result he also defaulted with his suppliers. He stopped his suppliers' payments, as a result, suppliers stopped supply. So he took out loans from the banks. This time he did his business with very good planning. He started to recover fast from his customers, but again some of his customers ran abroad without clearing his account. To revive his business, he asked for money from his relatives and continued his business. He asked for money from his siblings and friends; many of them gave him their life savings, for the sake of his business survival. But he failed again to meet his obligations. He was not able to return the money. His relatives also defaulted in the banks. Because some of them had given him money by taking a bank loan. So here you can see people get emotional and give their lives savings to the wrong person.

A Friend

My friend took out a loan for business but due to some reason, he wasn't able to do business immediately. So he put that money in his bank account to wait for an appropriate time. He thought that it would be better to keep that money in his savings account rather than return it. So he would not have to do loan formalities again. After some time, his relative asked him for money. He thought that he should help his relatives because he doesn't need money right now. So he gave them half of the amount. His relative promised him to return the amount within 2 months, but he broke the promise, and he gave him another date, and he continuously gave him the next date for one year. His relative returned him money after one year. He returned the money without interest, but my friend paid a heavy interest on the amount without utilizing and earning on that money. He lost many opportunities because of his relative's late repayment. He had the opportunity of doing many businesses, but he wasn't able to because he had given money. This is the worst scenario when a person lends money even after having a debt to himself. A person doesn't have the right to lend, loan money. There is a famous saying that 3 Fs are the best source of money, family, friends, and fools. Now you have to decide in which F you are falling.

Despite this, if a person has to lend money to someone, then 10 percent of his total savings can be lent to the closest one. In families, one can give free credit to each other, but cousins and uncles should avoid it.

We can see that if people do not manage money effectively, then they always remain on the losing side. The amount of money varies depending on the size of the mistake. It does not assure that a person will not make any mistake in his life. I have many examples of such people who have lost a lot of money without the knowledge of money management. People take a lot of debt for the expansion of the business, and later they fail. So it is clear that scaling on the base of a lot of debt is not a good strategy. Because this can disrupt the business. Lending money to someone may disrupt your life. **Never burn your home to save the other's house.**

Learn to say no

A person must learn the art of saying no to everyone. This is the most essential part of human life. Because everyone tries to use other people and their resources, and nothing is wrong with this. If you can use others' resources and money, it means you are smart enough to leverage other people's resources, but never let others use your resources. It doesn't mean that one should not help other people, but help should not cost your mental peace. It should not cost your resources, your opportunities, and your precious time. A yes person never succeeds in his life. People ask him for money, he says yes, takes it and suffers for money, loses opportunities to earn more money. People tell him to let's go to the party, he says ok let's go and wastes his precious time. Relatives call him for the renovation of their house, and he goes. His parents call him for small and unproductive work because he doesn't say no. To manage the money, it is important to say no to unnecessary expenses and unnecessary demands of friends and relatives. Unnecessary demands that steal the opportunities of earning money. So saying no is an art, you must learn it. People think that saying no is bad manners, but it is not bad manners, it is a critical art that everyone should have. This is the quality of an achiever.

Stop explaining and seeking reasons for your no. Dare to say no without any fake reason, tell them genuinely that you are not available for this work or the concerned favor, you have your priorities.

The Solution

I know your sister, brother, friend, business partners, and relatives are worth millions of dollars for you. But lend them money according to your worth, not according to their demand. Everyone deserves help, and you should help them but not at the cost of your peace. So I have a very simple method for you, to help your friends, family, and relatives.

If it is urgent and important and the person is trusted and close to you. Then you can give him 10% of your annual savings and tell him politely that this is all you have to give him, and you want to help him more but cannot. Always remember, this 10% help is for those people who can easily return it to you. Because this is not a donation, it is your pure savings, and it should be safe and secure in every situation. To do it, you need to keep your savings secret, so no one could force you to give them more than 10%. This is the simplest and the easiest way to avoid problems.

Mukesh Ambani has billions of dollars. And his brother is bankrupt, but Mukesh does not pay all of his brother's debt. Because he knows how to manage money, he knows how to keep money and how to grow wealth.

It is not that Mukesh Ambani is not a good brother. He is a good brother, he paid Anil Ambani's INR 500 Crore debt to save Anil from arrest. Probably this is the biggest aid given by a brother to a brother.

Keynotes

- Buying on credit means not cool, it means fool.
- Buying today and paying tomorrow is a drop of honey to drag you into the debt trap.
- Without need, buying a car on finance is the worst decision.
- Don't buy useless accessories because of credit card offers.
- Save personal loan options for emergencies.

- Limited use of business credit limits can make you a successful businessman.
- Always try to avoid lending money, the amount of the money only impacts the size of the mistake you make by lending money.
- You lose the opportunity to make money's best use, By lending money to others.
- Learn to say no, in case you have to lend money to help someone, then always help them with a little percentage of your savings.